Everything you always wanted to know about the French*
(*but were afraid to ask)

*Social-historical-humorous essay
on the French people*

France has neither winter nor summer nor morals, apart from these drawbacks, it is a fine country.
Mark Twain

Never doubt the courage of the French. They were the ones who discovered that snails are edible.

Doug Larson

God created France, the most beautiful country in the world with so much good in it, and ended up feeling guilty about it. He had to do something to make it fair. And so, he created the French people.

Janine di Giovanni

To all my compatriots,
whom I certainly make fun,
but always with love, affection, and kindness.

Contents

Foreword

You have in your hands a book whose main subject is to elucidate the nature and behavior of the French people, written by a Frenchy.

But who does he think he is? What is his legitimacy?

And if ever you are French, you may also wonder: what can he tell us about ourselves and our country that we don't already know?

Know thyself, as the wise Greek philosophers used to say. Introspection has many virtues. It allows us to better understand, and even sometimes excuse, some of our own behaviors and habits.

Hindsight and distance from oneself are often beneficial. We also usually say: "When I look at myself, I feel sorry. When I compare myself, I console myself."

To answer the question of legitimacy, I know France perfectly well... despite not having lived there for the last 25 years!

When I come back to my native country, I feel that it is my expatriate land. Everything is so different, so particular, so... French.

This country never ceases to amaze me, because it is simply fascinating.

Describing one's own country is a perilous exercise. However, one must recognize there is always something happening in France, whether a sporting event, a cultural one, a social event, a strike, or even, and unfortunately, the burning of one of its cathedrals.

If I hadn't been French, so much would I have loved to be!

There is so much to write about the French, but why?

Because they invented cinemas, cars, and radioactivity, but also the bra, the croque-monsieur, the garbage can, and dentures.

Because the French put Napoleon, Louis XIV, General de Gaulle, and Jacques-Yves Cousteau, Zinédine Zidane, and Tony Parker on the same pedestal.

Why did the French choose the rooster as their emblem while neighboring countries opted for powerful animals such as the eagle, bull, or lion?

A country whose citizens built a plane (Concorde) able to connect Paris and New York in four hours, but also had the wonderful idea of putting pianos in airports and turning a train station into a beautiful museum.

Because in France, a president can have a mistress, be dumped during his term of office, marry a woman several decades older than him, or even die in the middle of a sexual action.

France, this so-called ex-colonial empire, the only country in the world to exercise its sovereignty over all oceans.

Because the French can cumulate the titles of world champions in soccer, along with wine consumption and hours spent eating.

A country that has managed to transform a piece of clothing stored in the trunk of a car into a major symbol of a protest movement.

Because in France, we intrinsically like to rebel against everything: system, government, our employer, and we go so far as to go on strike preventively against a law that does not yet exist.

A country where food is so important that it is included in the intangible cultural heritage of UNESCO.

Because in France, depending on the region where you are, you greet each other with a kiss, two kisses, or sometimes even five.

France, a rainbow nation, multicultural, with a great mix of black, brown, and white people, but yet still struggling to assimilate it.

A country seen as the country of love and where the words "Voulez-vous coucher avec moi ?" are the most pronounced by foreigners.

Because the French express themselves in a language qualified as one of the sexiest, albeit with sounds so often considered animalistic: *coucou, quoi, oui…*

A country where the waiters in the café eternally wear bow ties while their clients dip a croissant into their coffee.

A people capable of swearing and wishing good luck with the same five-letter word (*merde*).

Because the French are capable of worshipping their king and cutting off his head, and after installing an emperor as a substitute, repudiating him by sending him into exile.

France, the country of wine, champagne, cognac, armagnac, calvados, pastis, and so many other elixirs of youth.

A country where artists transform urinals into works of art, build a glass pyramid in front of a century-old building, or split the sky of their capital with a steel tower.

All these aforementioned examples give a taste of the paradoxes, oddities, and zany, almost incoherent inventions and customs that I will refer to in the following pages.

I wrote this book with the ambitious goal of sharing curious facts about France and its citizens and trying to find an explanation.

I also compiled several funny anecdotes, all of which are true, bearing in mind that humor is an effective and particularly pleasant way of communication.

Over the course of this book, I'll take you on a virtual excursion to France in order to verify the veracity of its many clichés and stereotypes.

I also offer you a global reflection on the French lifestyle, which is so singular, atypical, and surprising, and transport you into the heart of an expatriated Gallic who makes fun of his country as much as he loves it.

Enjoy your reading and bon voyage to France!

Chauvinistic people who venerate their heroes... and sometimes also repudiate them

In France, we are extremely proud to be French, especially in front of foreigners; such a characteristic trait is what is commonly called chauvinism. Criticizing France is a crime of *lèse-majesté* if you are not French; on the other hand, the Gallic are the world champions of self-criticism, self-flagellation, or French bashing...

In short, one only has the right to criticize France if one is French!

Make sense of that if you can...

Coming back to my country, I sometimes criticized it out loud because of a strike that canceled my flight, or a "yellow vest" that delayed my appointment... and each time I was attacked by my compatriots: "You don't have the right to criticize, you don't live in France!" These same compatriots who, in a flash, will strongly vilify our common country, and often for identical reasons: "What a mess, another strike! Poor France..."

A similar observation can be made for foreigners who chose France as a place to live, and for whom any criticism of their country of asylum is most unwelcome.

Former President Nicolas Sarkozy is even credited with the now famous slogan: "France, either you love it or you leave it."

So, let me adjust my first statement: one only has the right to criticize France, but only if one is French, and only if one lives in France!

According to a recent survey conducted on a group of multi-national participants, France has the largest number of arrogant inhabitants in Europe. Even so, according to this survey, the French were the only ones to consider themselves as the most arrogant, while every other nation polled designated another country!

A nice way of admitting one's wrongs. It is wisely said that "a sin confessed is half forgiven."

But why is the myth (or perhaps reality) of French arrogance so well-known?

Well, there are a number of cultural discrepancies that could explain it.

If, in France, you enter a store without saying the magic word "Bonjour," followed by "s'il vous plaît," and you challenge the employee by asking, "What are you selling?"

Or even worse, if you fail to dominate the subtleties of the French language and the formal mode of address, by saying, for instance:

"Qu'est-ce que tu as à me vendre, toi?" (Hey, man. What do you have to sell?)

The answer will most likely not be the friendliest... This is because the French are usually very strict on the rules of courtesy.

Although Paris is one of the most visited cities in the world, the priority of the tourist is not quite the same as that of the capital's inhabitants. Parisian pedestrians are often in a hurry and are not inclined to help tourists looking for directions, and the waiters of bars and restaurants are often impatient when receiving orders.

And above all, there is the language barrier. Even if the trend is reversing with the new generations, many French people are still allergic to Shakespearean language.

So, if we don't understand each other, then how can we get along?

For example, when a couple of foreign tourists visiting France told a travel agency's employee: "We would like to go to Normandy with Aline," perplexed, the employee then asked them who this young woman was. The customers were annoyed by the travel agent's incompetence, and insisted, "Aline, you know... with everything!" until the unfortunate young man realized that he had to understand, "All In," that is to say, all included!

In a similar line of unfortunate confusions, another foreigner once went to the tourist office in Quiberon in Brittany to consult the opening hours of the Musée des Chiants. After making his request, the hostess kindly corrected him in these terms: "You mean the Musée des Chouans, I presume." *Chiant* is a very vulgar word whose meaning is something similar to *crap*, and *chouan* is the name given to the royalist insurgents who fought in Brittany.

The crap museum, if ever it exists, could be interesting to visit; however, I don't think it was what this tourist was looking for...

The French love their country so much (despite criticizing it so much) that sometimes they can come across as arrogant.

Further, when answering the question of another survey: what is your ideal country to live, work or study? The vast majority of those surveyed chose an exotic destination, while most French respondents answered... France!

Coming back to chauvinism, this powerful feeling of national pride, for the record, the word holds its origin from another Nicolas—Nicolas Chauvin. A soldier of the First Empire, he lost some fingers in a battle, along with a piece of skull (one wonders how could this has happened!). Despite this, he continued fighting and proudly defending his nation.

And French people are so chauvinistic!

A Swedish friend wisely pointed out to me that in France, we are very fond of this word. Our airline is called Air France, and the famous company Électricité... de France. The same is true for our gas company; our television channels (France 2, France 3); our former currency, the franc, a ship that made us famous—the France; and many newspapers: *Aujourd'hui en France, Jours de France, France Football.* The list is not exhaustive.

The first name *France* is also common. And there is even an actress with the pretty name Cécile de France, but she's Belgian. Too bad!

In Sweden, the national airline is called Scandinavian Airlines System, the currency the krona, and the electricity company Vattenfall. Obviously, my Swedish friend's remark is quite relevant.

Yes, yes. In France, we like that word.

And the most obvious example to illustrate my point is the Stade de France.
Once completed, this stadium destined to host the territory's major sporting events, among others, the 1998 World Cup football, had been the object of a nationwide consultation.
The country's leading minds, as well as a representative selection of compatriots, were invited to spend an entire weekend brainstorming in order to find a representative name for this place. The result of this exceptional brainstorming effort was extremely original since it resulted in the creation of the name "Stade de France"... Unbelievable!
The Parc des Princes, another Parisian sports stadium, had been named in a slightly more original way. Given that Saint-Denis is the city where the French kings rest in peace, an evocative name could have been the Garden of Kings...

Talking about kings, the last of them, for many French people, is... Johnny Hallyday.

Though I may surprise, or even shock many with this statement, it is enough to remember the emotion aroused by his death to realize the extent of the cult generated by the singer, who was, ironically, also of Belgian origin.

The whole country held its breath for days to pay tribute to this artist, who was adored by generations of fans. The media coverage was unprecedented, and even at the top level, a state funeral was organized.

My wife, in front of such a craze, could not believe her eyes, nor her ears. I could tell her that her compatriot, Julio Iglesias, would probably unleash similar passion in his native country... well no, the Spanish, like other peoples, as passionate as they are, are not as extreme as the French when it comes to venerating their stars.

And what about the cult devoted to General de Gaulle?

His name is associated to the first airport of the country, to the most emblematic square in Paris, to one of the most prestigious avenue of the French capital, and so many other honors.

Those honors are, nevertheless, well-deserved, if we remember the heroic actions of the general during the Second World War, while our Johnny Hallyday...

One must be Gallic to assimilate this kind of phenomenon!

We also have the annoying habit of eventually repudiating our heroes, and sometimes not until they pass away.

This is how Napoleon died after six years of exile on St. Helena, a tiny island lost in the middle of the Atlantic ocean, and so far away from his motherland, for which he had fought so hard. The English were the main party responsible for his exile. Proud of their last victory over the emperor at Waterloo, they found it suitable to send Napoleon to a place where he could no longer "harm the rest of the world." Although six years was more than enough time for a compatriot to rescue him, nobody even tried it.

General de Gaulle had an ungrateful exit from his political life, suffering a massive "no" from the French in the referendum he had submitted to them. This consultation did not concern his continuation as head of state, but was rather about a new law concerning the creation of regions and the renovation of the congress. Considerably offended by this result, de Gaulle assumed it was a personal failure. He died one year later.

And Johnny Hallyday fell in the esteem of so many of his fans for having disinherited (subject to tangible proof) his first two children to benefit his last two.

Being a hero in France is no easy feat!

In France, we don't have oil, but we have ideas.

This famous advertising slogan, born between the two oil crises of the 1970s, have been proven accurate when one considers the number of French inventions that have transformed our lives.

Gallic brains invented automobiles, airplanes, hot-air balloons, steamboats, calculating machines, internal combustion engines, bicycles, photography, cinema, micro-computers, smart cards, pencils, the metric system, and matches, to name but a few; however, they also invented the modern bra, the folding umbrella, aspirin, canned food, dry cleaning, the hair dryer, the sandwich maker, the dustbin, dentures, and the bidet!

The following list comprises several other noteworthy French individuals:

Parisian author Charles Perrault wrote the fairy tales of *Sleeping Beauty, Little Red Riding Hood, Puss in Boots, Cinderella, Bluebeard, The Master cat*, and *Little Thumb*.

The explorer Jacques-Yves Cousteau not only invented the scuba diving suit but also redacted a treaty for the global protection of Antarctica, which is still in force today.

The *Statue of Liberty*, an inspiring symbol of one of the most fascinating cities in the world, is a gift from the French, sculpted by Frédéric Auguste Bartholdi. In addition, the no less fascinating *Christ the Redeemer* of Rio de Janeiro is the masterpiece of the Parisian Paul Landowski.

Twenty-three centuries after their Greek versions, Baron Pierre de Coubertin had the brilliant idea to revive the Olympic Games.

Thanks to the devotion of Jean-François Champollion, the Egyptians were able to decipher the writings of their ancestors.

Ferdinand de Lesseps was the promoter of some of the most ambitious projects of his time: the Suez Canal and the Panama Canal.

Ambroise Paré and Antoine-Laurent de Lavoisier are considered to be the fathers of surgery and modern chemistry, respectively, while Robert Schuman and Jean Monnet are considered the fathers of Europe.

The Marquis de La Fayette played a crucial role during the American Revolutionary War on the side of American insurgents.

Many of the prophecies of the apothecary astrologer Nostradamus have been proven to be true more than five centuries later.

Louis Pasteur's research resulted in a miraculous vaccine that put an end to the dreadful plague of rabies.

Pierre and Marie Curie (first woman to win a Nobel Prize, and the only woman to win the Nobel Prize twice) conducted pioneering research on radioactivity.

Some French people have also been known for their devotion to several causes. For example:

The priest Abbé Pierre founded Emmaus, a movement to fight poverty and exclusion, which is still active today on all continents.

Sister Emmanuelle, the "little sister of the poor and the ragpickers," devoted her life to children in distress and the destitute, particularly in Egypt.

The comedian Coluche, after demonstrating his talent on stage, showed his generosity by creating *Les Restos du cœur,* an association distributing meals to the most needy, still active a few decades after its creation.

So many glorious Frenchies... and the list is far from complete.

Cock-a-doodle-doo!

By the way, why did the French choose the rooster as their emblem? Well, the origin came from a linguistic coincidence between the Latin words "gallus" (rooster) and "Gallus" (Gaul). Hence, it seems that the Romans mocked the Gauls by playing on the two terms. With the passing of time, the kings of France adopted the animal with the crest and the pretty plumage as the national emblem owing to its courage and its bravery. It is also worth pointing out that Spanish-speaking countries continue to call us roosters (gallos).

An eagle to represent Germany, a lion for England, a bull for Spain. We, the French people, chose the rooster! Perhaps because, as the comedian Coluche pertinently said: "The French have chosen the rooster as their emblem because it is the only bird that keeps on singing while walking in shit!"

While American superheroes have huge powers, impressive muscles, and fly through the air, the Gallic superhero wears a beret, a mustache, a cockade, and a tank top, and answers to the evocative name of *Superdupont*... and we are proud of it!

The cult movies of the inhabitants of France are not *Titanic, E.T., Avatar,* or any other blockbuster of this type, but rather comedies such as *Le père Noël est une ordure* (Santa Claus is a scumbag), *Le Gendarme de Saint-Tropez (the Troops of St. Tropez)* or *Les Bronzés font du ski* (The tanned are skiing), and we are also very proud of them!

Over the course of this book, I will recall other famous French people, including artists, writers and philosophers, but it is impossible not to mention Joan of Arc (Jeanne d'Arc), also a repudiated heroine. After years of struggle against the assailant from across the Channel, she was captured by her unscrupulous compatriots and sold to the English, who burned her alive, accusing her of being a sorceress.

What else can we say about her that we don't already know? Well, she was never called Jeanne of Arc during her lifetime; her first name was Johanne, but over time, her name was modernized to "Jeanne."

Her father's name was indeed d'Arc (related to the bridge), but in "the place" where she was born (Domrémy-la-Pucelle in the Vosges department), daughters were named after their mother, and although her mother was given the name de Vouthon (a village five kilometers from Domrémy-la-Pucelle), her offspring was nicknamed "Romée" in reference to a pilgrimage to Rome.

In other words, Joan of Arc's real name is Johanne Romée.

On the other hand, contrary to what is often thought, her nickname "the Virgin of Orleans" had nothing to do with her alleged virginity. At that time, the word virgin was primarily used to emphasize purity.

And Jeanne d'Arc, just like Charles de Gaulle, also had the honor of giving her name to a famous French aircraft carrier!

The Superdupont of the cartoonist Gotlib and the Gallic
rooster

"Voulez-vous coucher avec moi?": the myth and reality of the French lover

While visiting Egypt, at the foot of the pyramid of Cheops, the presumed tomb of the eponymous pharaoh, I answered a young guide who had asked my nationality with the autochthonous phrase:

"Oh, l'amour! Voulez-vous coucher avec moi?"

To which I replied, "Hey, young man. I am not such an easy boy!"

The tourists witnessing the scene in the first place laughed out loud! It appears that the words *love, fiancé, rendez-vous, coucher avec moi*, and *ménage à trois* are relentlessly linked to the image of the French.

We can't complain about it; since we are talking about love, it is a rather flattering prejudice.

But then why such fame? And what is the reason for such stereotypes? Why France is so often perceived as a libertine and romantic country?

I will attempt to explain why over the course of this chapter.

Summarizing France to Paris is a far too easy shortcut, but the French capital is perceived by many as "the city of love." As novelist Jules Renard once wrote, "Add four letters to Paris and you have the word: paradise."

A stroll along the banks of the Seine, a walk in the Luxembourg Garden, a visit to the Sacré-Coeur in Montmartre, a cruise on a bateau-mouche, and Cupid's magic is immediately at work.

Thus, Paris is the world capital of wedding proposals, but also of wedding photos!

Newly wed couples don't hesitate to pack their bags and pose triumphantly at the foot of the Eiffel Tower, and in turn, in front of the Arc de Triomphe.

Some of these lovers may remember the famous photograph by Robert Doisneau. Taken in the 1950s, the photo depicts a couple kissing passionately with the city hall in the background. A mythical and universally known cliché.

Many couples come to Paris to seal their love spiritually, and sometimes materially, baptizing a padlock and hanging it symbolically on a bridge of the capital. As a result, one of them, the Pont des Arts, crumbling under the weight of these utensils and deemed unsightly by some, had to swap its steel handrail for modern glass panels, making it impossible to hang the "padlocks of passion."

Lovers can console themselves with the *Wall of je t'aime*, located on the Montmartre hillock. This gigantic mural reproduces the sentence "I love you" on enameled lava tiles in no less than two hundred and fifty languages.

Which schoolboy has never engraved with a penknife the name of his first love? What teenager has not cut into the bark of a tree to inscribe his initials and those of the object of his desires in the middle of a heart pierced by an arrow?

The *Wall of je t'aime* is a tribute to these anonymous expressions of affection and is the new darling of couples visiting the French capital.

But Paris is also known for another kind of "love." The Bois de Boulogne, the Place Pigalle, and the numerous swingers' clubs of the city are fine examples of the libertine character of the French capital.

As a matter of fact, France has been notably pioneer in the field of libertinage. Its origin comes from a philosophical reaction against the moral constraints of the Church in the 16th century. The young libertines sought scandal and provocation through their writings and their attitudes, flouting all established rules. This was the time when Crébillon, Sade, and Laclos—true icons of debauchery—became famous.

On a lighter note, the Folies Bergère, the Lido, the Moulin Rouge, and the Crazy Horse have also reinforced the myth of Parisian cabarets with their shows with dancers so scantily clad.

However, one paradox to take into account is that although Paris may be qualified as the city of love, it is also one of the cities with the most divorced couples on our planet.

The French language is perceived by many foreigners as a very "sexy" language, which contributes to the myth of the *French Lover*.

As a Dutch friend wisely pointed out to me, adding a very explicit mimic, that to pronounce French properly, you need to put your mouth in a shape of a heart!

Anglo-Saxons, among others, love the accent of the Gauls when they speak English.

In this regard, a French woman was once the buzz on social networks when she said: "What you need in life is happiness."

This is a very honorable statement, since no one can deny that happiness is fundamental in everyone's life.

But the very pronounced French accent of the young woman radically transformed the meaning of the sentence, which was perceived as: "What you need in life is a penis."

A quote that does not have the same meaning, we must admit...

"Love" is the most pronounced word in the world, which is great news, since love should be the most important thing in our life.

But guess what? The origin of the word is... French.

"Se lover," which is the action of rolling up on oneself, is the basis of the English word, at a time when French was commonly spoken in England.

Still in the language of Shakespeare, the term *French kiss* is used to refer to a languorous kiss.

In my native Provence, the words "tongue soup" are commonly used, which is much less distinguished...

Apparently, the expression *French kiss* came just after the First World War, when American and English soldiers coming back home reported to their family the shocking practices of the French soldiers, who were apparently unfaithful and libertine, so far away from the romantic and puritanical ideals of American and English soldiers.

In line with what I just mentioned about the preponderance of love in France in all its forms, I should also remind readers that the election of Miss France is the most watched program in France. And moreover, French sales of women's lingerie and contraceptives are among the highest in the world!

The singer Antoine, in his *Elucubrations*, was quite right to sing: "To enrich the country, just put contraceptive pills on sale in the supermarket, oh yeah!".

Many men (and certainly women too) may still remember Brigitte Bardot wearing a white bikini, which immediately became a cult image from the movie *And God... created woman.*

I recall that the film was released in 1956, when France was still very puritanical.

Others have certainly more in mind when the actress no longer wears a bikini...

Anyway, this two-piece swimsuit is a Gallic invention and the work of a man who, noticing that women often lowered their bathing suits to get a better tan, had the idea of a light garment (to say the least), composed of a band for the top and two inverted triangles for the bottom.

For the record, the man in question, Louis Réard, had inherited a lingerie store from his mother near the Folies Bergère in the Pigalle area of Paris, and got the idea for the name bikini because at that time, on the Bikini Atoll in the Marshall Islands, there had been a nuclear explosion. Hoping that the impact of this new piece of fashion would be comparable to that of an atomic bomb, he went so far as to file a patent to protect his creation.

Nowadays, bikinis have become one-piece swimsuits on many beaches in France because of the "almost complete" style. And then there is the monokini.

My mother told me that when I was a child, observing "topless" women on a beach for the first time, I asked her an insightful question: "But don't these women have enough money to buy full bathing suits?"

Back in the summer of 1981, an outdoor poster campaign made headlines in France. The posters featured a young woman dressed in a single bikini, fists on hips, her back to the sea, and the shocking announcement: "On September 2, I remove the top."
On September 2, a second poster, almost identical to the first one, showed that the young woman had indeed taken off her swimsuit top.
But the advertiser didn't stop there. The series continued with a new announcement: "On September 4, I'm taking off the bottom."
And on September 4, a third and final advertisement showed the model with her swimsuit bottoms removed, but this time posing showing her back and with the slogan: "Avenir, the poster maker who keeps his promises".

Needless to say that this advertisement became totally cult throughout France, and still is...

I was lucky enough to study in the *city of love*.
With friends, we had developed many flirting strategies that were generally successful. One of these techniques involved getting close to a girl, holding a piece of paper in our hand, and asking her if she could lend us something to write on (during my student days, cell phones didn't exist).
As women usually have many accessories in their bag, and pens are one of them, once the pen was out of the bag, we would hand the paper to the lady, asking her nicely to write down her phone number. However, we never managed to get a single phone number!
Nevertheless, it's the perfect technique to break the ice, arouse curiosity, and trigger a laugh... and later on, during the evening, try once more to get the so desired phone number to take the date further.

A friend of us deeply fell in love of a young girl who, every Friday, would meet her girlfriends in a bar in the *Quartier Latin* of Paris. Our friend was also there each Friday, hiding himself in a corner of the bar, observing the eyes full of stars, the object of his fantasies. It would be a platonic relationship of several weeks, which he decided to end by taking action.

He had warned us that we were going to be the witnesses of his first steps.

After several beers ingested, in order to give himself strength, he finally got close to the girl, yet he could only pronounce a few words of a speech, which he had prepared long before.

"You are really, very, very beautiful."

Her answer was scathing, cruel, implacable, but at least she was honest:

"Maybe. Thank you, in any case, but I am also very, very married."End of the conversation.

Here is how the hope of a passionate romance is destroyed in the space of a few unfortunate seconds...

Needless to say that it was for us, present in the front row of this mishap, one of our most memorable laughs of all our student period.
Fortunately for our friend, the pain was short-lived since he managed to console himself the very next day, within the arms of a Breton woman, met with the powerful technique of the pen!

The "average Frenchman" is not the only one to be flirtatious. How can we not mention the preponderant place of love... among the presidents of the French Republic!

Already in the nineteenth century, there is a strong rumor of a "happy death" for the head of state, Felix Faure, in the presence of his mistress. According to legend, seeing her lover suffocating, the unfortunate woman called for help before running away, forgetting her corset on the top of the bed. The story goes that the priest who came for the extreme unction asked if the president still had his "connaissance," which has two meanings in

French——*mind* and *somebody you know*——and the president's bodyguard answered, "No, she has just fled by the service staircase."

Since the seventies, the French presidents have all been known for their sentimental antics.

Valery Giscard d'Estaing's penchant for pretty women was public knowledge. Moreover, he himself did not keep it secret, publishing a novel entitled *The Princess and the President*, based on a supposed romance with a woman who looked surprisingly like Diana Spencer.

A German journalist filed a complaint against Giscard d'Estaing, accusing him of putting a hand on her posterior after an interview given in 2018. The former president was only 92 years old when this happened!

François Mitterrand did not only show dynamism by speaking slang during an interview. During his term of office, the existence of a "hidden" daughter, the result of an extramarital relationship, came to light. At the funeral of the socialist president, the image of the three women of his life: his wife, his daughter, and her mother, united in grief, emoted the whole country.

When speaking about her husband, Bernadette Chirac admitted one day that "with women, it was a big rush." Faced with such a situation, the former first lady completely resigned when she said: "I told myself that this was the rule of game and my objective was to handle this with much dignity as possible."

For Nicolas Sarkozy, the opposite situation happened. He is part of a very select club of presidents who were dumped by their wives during their mandate. Yet, we used to say that women love power!

However, Sarkozy cleverly made up for it by marrying (again during his term of office) the singer and ex-model Carla Bruni, who gave him a daughter.

And for the first time in the history of the Republic, diapers and baby bottles invaded the first house of France!

Don't worry, the lull lasted only a short time up to the arrival of François Hollande in power, who had previously made news by leaving his long-time companion, Ségolène Royal, for a journalist from the magazine *Paris Match*. But in the middle of his mandate, Holland was spotted by a paparazzi when riding a scooter at night, along with his driver, on the way to meet his new conquest, who, incidentally, was eighteen years younger than him.

Dominique Strauss-Kahn has never been president, but he was very close to being one. While heading the powerful International Monetary Fund, an accusation of sexual assault in a New York hotel put an end to his ambitions for power. In the run-up to the election, Strauss-Kahn was the favorite in the polls.

French politicians are definitely incorrigible. Perhaps only Italy, with Berlusconi's antics, can possibly compete with France on this hot topic.

But all seems back to normal with President Emmanuel Macron. He appears a happily married man, transmitting a pleasant image of love. Some will not forget to point out that his wife, who used to be one of his teachers, is twenty-four years older than him, which is not so common...

Indeed, French politicians are really unique.

On a lighter note, we can also notice that many poets, novelists, and philosophers have been doing a great job at spreading the idea of French Romanticism.

How to remain insensitive in front of those masterpieces:

"My father gave me a heart, but you made it beat."
— Honoré de Balzac

"The world thirsts for love: you will come to quench it."
— Arthur Rimbaud

"We spend half of our life waiting for love, and the other half leaving those that we loved."
— Victor Hugo

"Love is a fabric woven by nature and embroidered by imagination."
— Voltaire

"Only one person is missing, and the whole world seems depopulated.
— Alphonse de Lamartine

"Love is a wafer that must be broken in two in front of an altar, and swallowed together in a kiss."
— Alfred de Musset

"Love is the miracle of civilization."
— Stendhal

"I won't say what reasons you have for loving me. You have none. The reason to love is love."
— Antoine de Saint-Exupéry

"Reason speaks, but Love sings."
— Alfred de Vigny

"Love is incurable."
— Marcel Proust

And after the pen, the voice!
In spite of the tough competition from Anglo-Saxon singers, many French artists have succeeded in making their works a worldwide success, and have thus contributed to promote France as a lyrical country.
The mythical *La Vie en rose* or *Hymne à l'amour* by Édith Piaf have crossed generations. The touching *Comme d'habitude* (*My way*) by Claude François is the most covered song in history. Jacques Brel and his magnificent *Ne me quitte pas* remain the symbol of French romanticism. Yes, but the problem is that Brel was not French, but Belgian. Again, what a pity!

To close this chapter dedicated to love in "the French way," this last anecdote will probably leave you voiceless.

When living in Marseille, I was keen on organizing dance parties. One day, while walking in a street with a Parisian cousin who had come to spend a few days to visit me, we met a friend. I took the opportunity to invite this friend to my next party, praising it in the following terms: "I am sure you will really enjoy the evening. Very beautiful girls of Marseille will be there." But as I finished the last sentence, I remembered that my friend had a girlfriend, so I rectified my speech a little: "But please come with your girlfriend; she is obviously more than welcome." The Marseillais immediately replied to me with his lovely accent from the south of France: "Gaspard, when you go to a restaurant, do you really bring your sandwich?"

My cousin could not believe his eyes... nor his ears! More than twenty years later, he still talks to me about this.

But that's not all.

The following Saturday, the party did take place, and indeed my friend came... albeit without his girlfriend.

But the last sentence, which had a permanent impact on my cousin, who acted as the DJ during the party, was when our Marseillais friend asked him to put some slow music to dance closely with the girls, using the following words: "Hey, man. When are you going to put some broken zipper music?"

The final touch.

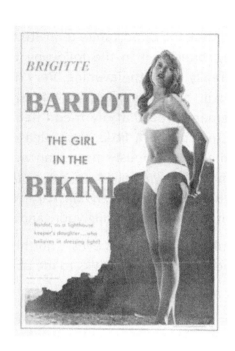

Brigitte Bardot wearing a bikini on the front page of a
foreign magazine. Oh là là!

The language of Molière, but also of Hugo, Corneille, Voltaire, Baudelaire, etc.

German is defined as the language of Goethe, Italian is immediately associated with the writer Dante, Spanish remains the language of Cervantes, and English is linked to Shakespeare.

But what about French? The language of Molière, Voltaire, Corneille, Racine, Hugo, Verlaine, Rimbaud, Baudelaire... and so many others.

So lucky, so rich!

But before being popularized by illustrious writers and poets, the language of Descartes took a winding path.

In order to identify its origin, we must go back to two millennia ago, or precisely, to the height of the Gallic War (from 58 BC to 51 BC), when the south of the Rhine territories became Roman provinces.

At that time, the Gauls spoke Gallic, a Celtic origin language. The Romans, of course, spoke Latin, albeit in a "vulgar" derivative, with notable differences in the written language, similar to those that we can observe today between spoken and written Arabic.

The mixture of the two languages, Latin and Gallic, is at the origin of French.

But since Gallic was not much transcribed, as a consequence, it lost strength. Nowadays, in the French dictionaries, only hundreds of words still have Gallic roots.

When Clovis unified the Frankish peoples in the 5th century, to get the support of the eminent Gallo-Roman families, he adopted their language, Gallo-Roman, and at the same time, their religion, Catholicism. It is thanks to this unification, among other events, that we find numerous strange contractions in the French language, such as: œ of nœud, sœur, or cœur, for example.

But the real birth certificate of the language of Molière took place three decades later, during the time of the "Oaths of Strasbourg." Signed by the grandsons of Charlemagne, this document is considered the first official document of French, and had not much to do with the language spoken today. Here is an excerpt: *"Pro Deo amur et pro christian poblo et nostro commun salvament."*

Sounding rather like a *lorem ipsum*, this meaningless placeholder text is commonly used for previewing layouts and visual mockups!

From the 10th century onwards, the Oïl or Oc languages (*oïl* and *oc* meaning *yes*) appeared mainly in the northern half of the country, whereas today they are mainly spoken in the south. They are commonly considered dialects of French. Then, during the Renaissance, with the invention of the printing press, it was necessary to "fix" and unify a jargon for the rising book industry. This is how the French language, as we know it today, first appeared.

At the beginning of the 17th century, the French language became so popular that it displaced Latin as the official dialect of the dominant courts in Europe. It then became the prime diplomatic language.

A relatively unknown fact is that French was the official language in England for over three hundred years!
After the country's invasion in the Middle Age by William the Conqueror, Duke of Normandy, the Anglo-Norman dialect became the most widely spoken on the other side of the Channel.
This is why some English words have French roots, such as cat (chat) or carrier (charrier).
From this heritage, the motto of the British monarchy has remained Gallic: *Dieu et mon droit*, as well as the motto of the chivalric Order of the Garter: *Honni soit qui mal y pense*. Those French quotations still appear on the coat of arms of the United Kingdom.
It's only in 1336 that English came back as the official language for legal proceedings and of the British universities.

Why was French so popular?

Apart from its proximity to Latin, historians point out the assets of French being a "logical and precise" language.

Today, French is one of the six official languages of the United Nations, the second most studied language in the world, and remains one of the most widely spoken. French high schools, *alliances françaises*, and other similar institutes contribute to this emancipation.

What is perhaps less well known is that Paris has lost its status as the leading French-speaking city in the world since Kinshasa has taken over this honorary title.

Abidjan, Montreal, Casablanca, Yaoundé, Douala, Antananarivo, Dakar, and Algiers follow in a ranking where one has to go back further and further to find another city from France.

Fifty-one countries and territories have Victor Hugo's language as their official or co-official language. This is a world record!

Since I am expatriate, whenever I go back to my country, I am always surprised to observe the changes in my own language.

Recently, while listening to my 15-year-old nephew from Paris conversing with one of his friends, I heard him use the expressions *badass*, *kiffer*, *gadjo*, *baptou*, *mazel tov*, *swag*, and *smile*; however, I could only understand one word out of four.

A powerful decoder is now needed to capture the conversations of today's youth! Traditional dictionaries the likes of *Larousse* should have some worries...

It is also worth underlining a strange mixture of Arabic (kiffer), Jewish (mazel tov), gypsy (gadjo), African (baptou), and Anglophone (smile) words, in the vocabulary adopted by French youth.

As the world becomes ever more global, such linguistic trends are only likely to increase, especially when considering that France is a truly multicultural country. I will come back to this subject later on in the book.

In 1985, François Mitterrand made the headlines when he showed off his youthful spirit by quoting the word *chébran* ("super cool" in french slang) during an interview. When questioned by the journalist, the ex-president, admitted that he also spoke slang during his childhood.

The word *chébran,* dear to François Mitterrand, is somewhat out of fashion today, but it is not the only one.

In my parents' youth, they used to say "I am flirting (*flirter* in French) with someone." In my youth, the expression "dating" (*sortir avec*) was used. Nowadays, young people say that they have hooked up (*pécho*), or even worse, they have *kuf* (inverse of *fuck*, or *ken* in French).

Other times, other customs...

In the nineties, we used to say: "Il se la joue un maximum" (He's playing the hard to get to get), when referring to a person who was too proud of himself or "Il a fait fort" (He did great) to describe a person who succeeded in doing something improbable. Such wording is no longer in use, and has been replaced by a number of strange expressions, such as "ça envoie du lourd" (something big is sent), or "il a craqué son slip" (he broke his underwear).

We, French people, are sometimes so hard to understand!

The term "It's in our DNA" is no longer applied in a medical context, but it is often thrown around by politicians and entrepreneurs.

The expression "C'est une tuerie" (it's a kill) refers more to a delicious dish rather than a bloody massacre.

The expression "Péter un câble ou les plombs" (fuse or blowing off steam) no longer has anything to do with an unfortunate electrical manipulation; nowadays, it is used to describe somebody who has lost their mind.

The adjective "juste" (just) has become a language tic, but no more used in its "right" meaning. While watching French television, my children have pointed out that it is even the word most often pronounced by singers, actors, presenters, and columnists who appear on the small screen.

They say that the truth comes out of the mouths of children...

All this is just incredible!

The French language has been enriched not only by its cultural diversity, but also by the evolution of its society.

In France, we all know that a *bobo*, a contraction of *bourgeois-bohemian*, is an individual from a well-to-do class, but who votes for left wing parties by principle.

The *quincado* is between 45 and 60 years old yet still acts and thinks like a teenager.

The expression "chic-ouf" (great-great) is associated with the vocabulary of the elder generations: "Great the grandchildren come, great they leave."

The phonetic shortcut *askip* is used to avoid pronouncing the words: *à ce qu'il paraît* (so it seems).

The use of texting, WhatsApp, and other messaging apps on cell phones has introduced a new form of language, at least shortened, very often made with English roots and composed of acronyms.

French young people also write *OMG, WTF,* or *YOLO,* when we used to write *Carpe diem* for this last one.

MDR (mort de rire) is the French equivalent of LOL (*Laughing Out Loud).* Regarding this last expression, a joke became famous on the web, telling the story of a woman who sent the following text message to all her contacts: "Grandpa is dead, LOL," thinking that this acronym stood for *Lots Of Love,* until her son pointed out that she had just announced to all of them: "Grandpa is dead, it's super funny."

So, beware of the incorrect use of this modern way of communicating... LOL!

In the south of France, for some years now, people have been calling each other "fatty man," even if they are very skinny. This is a very strange interjection, considering that in the nineties, people used to call each other "blond man," even if they had dark hair or were bald.

Still in the South of France, the expression *"c'est de l'enculage de mouches en vol"* (it's fucking flies while they flying) can definitely be very shocking because of its symbolism.

Nowadays, the French also often say the distinguished expression: *"Faut que je me sorte les doigts"* (I need to get my fingers out) in a context of a need for reaction. When they are very tired, they also say *"J'ai la tête dans le cul"* (my head is in my ass).

So chic, so class... What happened with the French delicatessen?

When I return to my own country, over the last few years, I have noticed that the expression *"pas de soucis"* (no worries) has become one of the favorites of my compatriots. From the baker whom I had given too much change to the mechanic who repaired the wheel of my motorcycle, each time I received in return a nice "pas de soucis." It is definitely a benevolent expression, similar to the Swahili formulation *hakuna matata*.

"Ça coûte un bras" (it costs an arm) is also a very common expression nowadays. Still, it's a strange way of associating a member of our body with goods that we buy or sell.

In a far more vulgar manner, some people also say *"ça m'a coûté une couille"* (it cost me a ball).

Once again, we take up this annoying tendency to give a market value to a part of our anatomy.

A "Charming" allegory, however...

Many French words and phrases have crossed borders. "...Et voilà" is regularly used by English speakers to end their words, and the word *chic* was not only popularized by a song.

The English have found nothing better than the expression "déjà-vu" to refer to a situation that is déjà-vu!

The words au pair, rendez-vous, vis-à-vis, and brunette can be found in many languages, but also fraud, femme fatale, coup d'état, and faux pas, which are a little less glorious!

Further, the words C'est la vie, Grand Prix, boutique, chef-d'œuvre, prêt-à-porter, also have a very honorable international career.

But the French do return the compliment by using many anglicisms: weekend, slow, standby, brunch, people, smile, scoop, speed, my life, girly, burn out, overbooked, overdose, cluster are now words of the French dictionary! And beware, new ones are coming, such as millennial, black bloc, pure player, and unfortunately, bullying, a word we wish we had never heard.

What about the famous expression "oh là là," an interjection that entirely characterizes the Gallic people. It is the "Swiss Army knife" expression that can be used in any circumstance, whether in a sad context: "Oh là là, I'm sorry for you," or in a joyful connotation: "Oh là là, I'm deeply happy."
These are frequently the first words in French that people learn, the ones they remember best, but also the last ones they understand!
Indeed, who can really explain what "oh là là" means?

French is one of the languages with the most exceptions in its spelling. When I tell my foreign friends that dictation contests are organized at the national level, and that very few people succeed in presenting a copy without mistakes, they don't believe their ears. Once again, we are talking about exceptions!

I shared an apartment with an Italian who once told me that the French language was the most "animalistic." And why is that, I asked him? He said that each time he listened to my conversations with French friends, sounds more akin to animals than humans were coming out of my mouth: *coucou, quoi, ou, ouf, aï, oui...*

In retrospect, he had a point... not to mention that some of the favorite expressions of the Frenchies are: "C'est chouette" (literally, "it's an owl," which means it's great), "*Oh la vache*" ("it's a cow," meaning "so surprising"), and "*Nom d'un chien*" ("in the name of a dog," meaning "so impressive").

To any French readers, I suggest we do our best to preserve our nice language because, as the slogan of a famous (French, of course) cosmetic brand goes, "It is well worth... *et voilà!*"

The very French coat of arms of... the United Kingdom.

Fashion and art:
"the French cultural exception"

The scene takes place in New York in 1917. In a prestigious art gallery, a man exhibits a work entitled *Fountain*.

So far so good, except that this *fountain* was previously purchased in a plumbing and sanitary store. It is a simple porcelain urinal, no less.

Fountain is considered to be the most controversial artwork of the 20th century. The artist in question is French; his name is Marcel Duchamp, and with him, contemporary art was born.

A century later, the jet set stars are snatching up the works of another Gaul, Richard Orlinski, and in particular, a King Kong in tinted resin, pounding his chest with his fists.

Between Duchamp's bidet and Orlinski's monkey, time has passed, but France remains a country where art and culture play a crucial role, even if sometimes we may not see the value of some masterpieces at first...

As a symbol that can be seen as arrogance, people in France talk about the "French cultural exception." Arrogance, because by playing on words, some could interpret that the French culture is exceptional!

But, as it is well known that the French are not arrogant at all (...), there is no doubt.

Arrogant or not, France had been the first country in the world to include a Ministry of Culture.

It was the writer, adventurer, and journalist André Malraux who was entrusted with this heavy task back in 1959. And he was the one who had the idea to take concrete actions in order to support the French artistic creation.

Those measures were based on the noble idea that cultural works should not be considered as a commercial goods, and, consequently, its trade had to be protected by certain rules other than those of the market law.

A beautiful ideology, which can be nevertheless expensive for taxpayers...

Any French citizen pays a yearly fee to finance public television and radio channels. But in the 21st century, taking into account the extensive private audiovisual offer, do we still need public channels?

The government may argue those public channels ensure impartial, quality information, without depending from advertisement revenue. But thanks to their public status, these channels depend directly on each government in power, which legitimately raises some questions about their impartiality...

And that is not all, since those public entities are also partially financed by advertising, thus contradicting the revenue free argument.

Another example: with more than 250 movies released each year, France is the leading European producer of seventh art, which contributes greatly to the nation cultural influence. Nevertheless, those movies are mostly financed by the state. In other words, French people pay twice for their local movies: first with their taxes, and then when they buy their cinema ticket.

At the same time, it is crucial to keep a certain legitimacy when it is on your country that is taking place the world's leading film event, *the Cannes film festival*.

Also, we should not forget that we owe the invention of the cinematograph, this ingenious machine showing photographic views in motion, to a French brotherhood—the Lumière brothers.

And on top of that, numerous French films have been internationally successful. From Luc Besson's Hollywood blockbusters to more intimate movies, such as *The Artist, La Môme, or Intouchables*.

It's the French touch!

The Frenchies love going to movie theaters, but also like to visit exhibitions and museums, and they are not the only ones.

More than sixty million people visit France's museums every year. The Louvre alone welcomes more tourists every year than India, Morocco, or Argentina!

People come to admire the *Mona Lisa*, the *Venus de Milo*, but also the fabulous treasures of Mesopotamia, Egypt, or ancient Greece.

A question can be asked: how did these masterpieces end up in France? Why, for instance, is the most famous of them, the *Mona Lisa,* not exhibited in an Italian museum?

Well, because she came to France by her own means!

It was transported by its author, Leonardo da Vinci, who made the one-way trip from Italy to France in 1516. The Florentine had found a patron and protector in the person of King Francis I, who was fascinated by his genius. The sovereign gave him a castle and named him "the king's first painter, engineer and architect," with an annual pension until his death, also in Gallic lands...

This is why the *Mona Lisa* has French identity papers.

Van Gogh was Dutch, but just like Leonardo da Vinci, spent a long time in France! The artist, who according to legend never sold any painting in his lifetime, scoured the countryside of Arles, Saint-Rémy-de-Provence and Auvers-sur-Oise, whose landscapes inspired most of his works.

More recently, Pablo Picasso, fleeing the Spanish civil war, found refuge in the capital of ancient Gaul. The magnificent Guernica was even painted in a Parisian attic. There is a tale that in occupied Paris, on a visit to his studio and in front of the Guernica painting, a Gestapo officer once asked him, "Did you do this?" to which Picasso replied, "No, you did."

The Venus of Milo, one of the greatest masterpieces of the Hellenistic period, landed in France after a most incredible story. A farmer from the island of Milos (hence its name), while digging the foundations to build a wall around his field, discovered a cave surrounding the famous statue. A group of French sailors staying on the Greek Cycladic island heard about the discovery and told their superiors about it. An offer was quickly sent to the local authorities to buy the statue to bring it to France. However, in the meantime, the farmer had sold the Aphrodite representation to a Greek official, who took it into a ship at the exact moment the French were returning with cash in hands. However, upon seeing the object of their desire leaving for a cruise, they were not amused to say the least. There followed an extremely tough negotiation that the French sailors ended by winning.

History does not tell whether the bust was orphaned of its arms since this battle, but in any case, we may have elucidated the origin of the French expression: "it cost an arm," for it was precisely two arms for the statue!

Regarding the question, "What is the oldest monument in Paris?" One would be tempted to answer the Lutetia arenas or the Cluny baths, both of them dating from the Gallo-Roman era; however, there is a catch. It is the obelisk of the Place de la Concorde that enjoys this title, although the monument is not really Parisian.

With its three thousand two hundred years of history, the monument proudly stands on one of the most emblematic squares of the capital, Place de la Concorde. Far from the temple of Luxor, its original birthplace, it is the result of a beautiful gift made by Egypt to France. It traveled nearly three years to arrive at destination in 1830 aboard a ship named The Luxor, of course, specially built for this purpose.

But France not only imported foreign works; the country also has its own batch of artists.

Some Gallic painters marked their place in art history, particularly the impressionists. On top of that, they are representative of the non-conformist attitude so characteristic to the French. The impressionist movement even made a crucial break with the academic art. Painting an impression rather than a reality, what an amazing idea. Painting something existing, living, but freely recreated according to his own vision, sensitivity, and interpretation.

Among many others, this is what Monet, Renoir, Sisley, Pissarro, Cézanne, Degas, Manet did brilliantly.

Impressionist painting remains one of the most fascinating periods in modern art history, and the genre is often considering the favorite of the public.

The French sculptor Auguste Rodin was in the worthy tradition of his rebellious compatriots, breaking usual standards. Rodin is even considered the father of modern sculpture. *The Thinker* is one of the most famous works in the art world, but not only; the statue is often used as an image to represent philosophy.

His work "Walking Man" might be less famous, but it made the headlines when it became public. It represents a man in motion, but without a head and arms. The artist, who was passionate about antiquity, wanted to pay homage to the statues, which, like the Venus de Milo that we mentioned, lost some limbs along the way, but whose beauty remained unharmed. The sculptor's detractors did not understand his intention. Some went so far as to declare that the production of such a work "had neither tail nor head." I invite you, dear readers, to corroborate these statements by carefully observing the photograph at the end of this chapter.

Nevertheless, despite losing its limbs, the statue remains magnificently elegant and has inspired a great number of artists.

And since we are mentioning elegance, if I write that France is "the country of elegance," I will certainly be called arrogant and chauvinistic. But the fact is that many people around the world share the same opinion. And even if they don't share this point of view, they may nonetheless be consumers of French elegance!

The famous minister of Louis XIV, Jean-Baptiste Colbert, once said: "Fashion is to France what the gold mines of Peru are to Spain." Talking about fashion in the 17th century and comparing it to the precious metal says a lot about its importance.

At that time, the splendor of Louis the Great's court in Versailles was admired and imitated by the whole of Europe. High society ladies visited Paris mainly to shop, as French tailors had the reputation of being eminently talented and their creations extremely sought after.

One woman, Rose Bertin, had the audacity to create her own fashion house at the corner of rue du Faubourg-Saint-Honoré. A rare audacity, since she was the only woman do so. Queen Marie-Antoinette took her under her wing, and she became the court's fashion designer, with the unofficial title of "Minister of Fashion."

At the same time, the first fashion magazine, *Mercure galant*, was released. And the trend never stopped growing.

Under the First Empire (i.e., just after the French Revolution), Paris was already the temple of fashion with more than 2400 tailors listed!

All those facts form the roots of this flattering reputation for France, and over time, Paris has only strengthened its unofficial title of "fashion capital."

In the top position of elegance, there is *haute couture*. It is even a legally protected trade name stemming from a 1945 law.

To be qualified as a "house of haute couture," the criteria for membership are very specific: work done by hand in the workshops of the house, two annual shows in the calendar of haute couture, a minimum number of passages per show (at least twenty-five), the use of a certain area of fabric, etc.

It is easy to understand why there are only a dozen or so of these prestigious Parisian fashion houses left, and why they are almost all loss-making.

So, what's the point of doing a time-consuming and costly activity?

Because haute couture is, first and foremost, a showcase for the image of a brand, which will then be marketed as accessories, perfumes, and ready-to-wear fashion, either directly or through licenses, it is extremely profitable.

And so, Christian Dior, Yves Saint Laurent, Pierre Cardin, André Courrèges, Christian Lacroix, Jean-Paul Gaultier, and Thierry Muglers are among the best known common names in the world and the most worn, whether for clothes, bags, or perfumes.

Most commonly men's names, but if there is one woman who understood perfectly how the system worked, before anyone else, it is Gabrielle, better known as "Coco" Chanel. The renowned couturier, is not only a symbol of French elegance, but she also was the first to launch her own perfumes.

Just like the novelists, artists' affairs often provided her with sources of inspiration. Thus, it is surprising to observe that the shape of her famous perfume, number 5, looks like a flask of vodka, and as legend has it, was inspired by an affair that Coco had with a Russian, a casual cousin of the final tsar!

Coco Chanel is considered by many as the most influential fashion designer of all time. When ladies were still wearing only skirts or dresses, she made the female trouser popular.

Today, almost every woman has a little black dress hanging in her closet. This is an invention of Coco Chanel, who one said: "A woman does not have to be beautiful, she must only believe it."

The sailor top, the white sweater with stripes so dear to Jean-Paul Gautier, was also born in the workshops of the artist, inspired by the sailors uniforms after a trip to a coast of France.

As the designer once stated, "My life didn't please me, so I created my life."

And indeed she did.

After this flattering description of French elegance and its ambassadors, I will be a little more critical.

There is, in particular, one artistic field where France is left behind—contemporary music.

The golden age of Edith Piaf or Jacques Brel, who, as I wrote earlier, was not Gallic. Given that this period ended long ago, French music is nowadays popular, mainly and only in... France.

As an example, the song *Voyage, voyage* by the artist Desireless is one of the best sold French records of the last thirty years.
Though the chorus is certainly catchy, and the melody pleasant, when competing with artists the likes of Adele, or Justin Bieber, there is still a long way to go!

The "mythical" Gallic bands like Indochine or Téléphone had their glory days, but mainly within the borders of France. The comparison with any famous Irish or British band is not even possible.

This can be blamed on the French language, given that is most likely less melodious than English, but it is also a question of culture and gender.

Nowadays, the most popular French-speaking singers are no longer French, whether they are men (Stromae) or women (Céline Dion).

Pianist Richard Clayderman, whose real name is Philippe Pagès, remains the most successful French musician abroad in recent decades, but his style as a "variety concert performer" is far removed from the standards of pop music. And rarely do we hear his voice...

Coincidentally, many other French pop music celebrities do not sing, since they are either disc jockeys, such as

David Guetta, or electronic music bands, such as Daft Punk, through whom we can notice the typically Gallic originality, since totally hidden under futuristic helmets, the public does not know their face, which contributes to their myth.

So, to resume my point, unless we naturalize Céline Dion or Stromae, which will make us very popular again with our Canadian and Belgian friends, we will need to wait a little longer to enjoy listening to the voice of an International French star.

Although France has few famous pop artists, the music of the nation is celebrated at least once a year in many countries, thanks to an idea that was born on French soil.

In 1982, Minister of Culture Jack Lang, under the presidency of François Mitterrand, came up with a brilliant initiative—to organize an event intended to encourage professional and amateur musicians to perform in streets and public spaces across France. All this would be accompanied by the wordplay slogan: *Faites de la musique!* Wordplay because party (*fête*) and make (*faites*) have the same pronunciation.

Since then, every June 21st (a date chosen because it often coincides with the summer solstice), music concerts of all kinds take place all over France. But not only, since the concept has also been adopted by more than 120 countries, and the list continues to grow each year.

In France, what we lack in famous rock bands, we make up in ideas!

The man who walks by Rodin,
a statue that leaves viewers deep in thought.

The ubiquitous role of cuisine in French society

Like a few lucky young Frenchies, I spent a few summers overseas to improve my English. One year, my host family was so religious that before every meal, they all stood around the table and said a prayer.

The patriarch of the household once asked me if my family had the same ritual—to pray before eating. I told him that we didn't because we were French; instead, we trusted our cooking.

The story is funny, but to be quite honest with you, it never happened, even if I would have loved to make this joke in such a situation.

However, this little lie helped me to introduce this chapter on the fame of Gallic gastronomy by serving it on a plate!

If we were to ask foreigners what they like best about France, "its cuisine" would probably be among the first things mentioned. French gastronomy is so prestigious that it even enjoys the privilege of being included in UNESCO's representative list of the intangible cultural heritage of humanity.

Now that is truly a recognition that can be tasted. Dinner is served!

Undeniably, gastronomy is associated with the French way of life. According to a recent study conducted by the OECD, on average, the Gauls spend more than two hours a day eating. No other country can do better. This is more than double the time spent by the Americans, the inventors of *fast food*, and rightly so.

Another statistic that speaks for itself: for 91% of the French people, their favorite discussion is about food, placing it far ahead of music, cinema, or soccer. In fact, only wine discussions come close to competing with those on food.

In France, the gastronomic culture is so strong that it is undeniable.

We can wonder where and when the origin of this "vice" lies, since gluttony is one of the seven deadly sins, as we must remember.

Anyone who has read the comic strip *Asterix the Gaul* must certainly remember the pantagruelian banquets that concluded each episode. As a matter of fact, French cuisine is mainly rooted in Roman food culture.

At that time, of course, we were still far away from pizzas and macaroni, but the influence of the Transalps on the French was fundamental, in no small part due to their simple and refined cuisine, very avant-garde for its time.

The French really started to be famous for their gastronomy during the Middle Ages. Guillaume Tirel, known as *Taillevent*, head chef to King Charles V, had a lot to do with it. Tirel revolutionized cooking by integrating vegetables, spices, and other ingredients brought back from the New World by the explorers. We owe him *the*

Viandier, the first recorded recipe book, which was already a great success at that time.

It was not in the time of the Romans, but at the end of the Middle Ages, that gigantic banquets, such as those that Obelix is so fond of, appeared. According to the writings, the food was not only highly decorated, but also copiously seasoned thanks to the systematic use of spices, the latter often causing collateral damage to stomachs...

The inflection point that took French gastronomy into another dimension was during the reign of king Louis XIV.

In the heart of Louis the Great's court, chefs vied with each other in effort and ingenuity for the pleasure of the monarch and his entourage. One of them in particular will forever be remembered for his cuisine—the pastry chef, caterer, steward, and head waiter François Vatel. A perfectionist to the core, Vatel has gone down in history for having committed suicide during a reception for the king, fearing that he would not be able to satisfy the three thousand guests because of a late delivery of the day's catch!

We usually say that it is the kings who made France (unless one is a seasoned republican). In any case, they have a lot to do with the advent of its gastronomy, at least in an indirect way.

A few centuries later, the globe-trotting chef Auguste Escoffier (1846-1935) allowed Gallic cuisine to spread throughout the world, successively expatriating himself to England, Switzerland, and the United States. His *Culinary Guide*, containing more than five hundred recipes, is the basis of modern cooking and remains the main coffee table book of many chefs of our time. Escoffier is also the father of the concept of brigades, organizing and rationalizing the tasks of the kitchen help.

French gastronomy has reinvented itself, with what has been called *nouvelle cuisine.*
This trend was born in the seventies, under the impulse of the gastronomic critics Henri Gault and Christian Millau, founders of the eponymous guide.
The objective of this innovative concept was to rediscover the fundamentals of cooking: simplicity, respect for the product, and a return to its flavor.
In order to do this, chefs drastically changed the way they cooked, lightening their menu, eliminating sauces, reducing cooking, and favoring creativity.
For the record, the term *nouvelle cuisine* was inspired by the *new wave* of French filmmakers of the 1960s and the *new novel*, a literary movement that was very popular at the same time.
That said, in our society, which is, fortunately, becoming more and more supportive and responsible, some of the aberrations of the *new cuisine* (which are no longer as new), specifically its minimalist portions that are sometimes charged at golden prices, are entitled to be shocking...

And we have gone even further.

In 1988, thanks to the scientific work of Frenchman Hervé and his Anglo-Hungarian counterpart Nicholas Kurti, molecular gastronomy was born.
Its objective is to research the physical and chemical phenomena that occur during culinary transformations. In other words, it's about watching what's happening at the

molecular level in a meat broth, or studying the evolution of the color of green vegetables during their cooking.

This discipline, usually practiced by scientists, is actually performed by cooks.

To do so, chefs use utensils similar to those used by doctors (syringes, capsules, tubes), ingredients that are more common in laboratories than in kitchens (powders, gelling agents, thickeners, emulsifiers) and techniques that are more appropriate to scientific books than to recipe ones (molecular cooking, dehydration, etc.).

The "food study" phase of the new cuisine, which was so innovative at the time, has largely been surpassed. And today's chefs have become true molecular alchemists!

How far we have strayed from the Gallic and medieval banquets of the day...

After this historical and scientific parenthesis, let's talk about the essential: the typical dishes of French cuisine.

There are so many (don't forget I am French, and hence fairly chauvinistic) that we would need another book to review them. However, let's mention twenty of the most famous ones: tartiflette, gratin dauphinois, coq au vin, boeuf bourguignon, pot au feu, quiche lorraine, crêpe, steak tartare, cassoulet, shepherd's pie, blanquette de veau, andouillette, roast chicken, ratatouille, pissaladière, frog's legs, bouillabaisse, escargots de Bourgogne, daube, sauerkraut.

It's interesting to point out that the regions of France are well represented in these dishes: from Lorraine where the quiche, from the South-West and its cassoulet, including the Breton crepe, the beef bourguignon, and the Savoy tartiflette.

And the French have never hesitated to travel miles and miles just for the pleasure of their palate. Thus, they are responsible for inventing gastronomic tourism.

A famous tire manufacture was most aware of this, if you know what I am referring to...

Indeed, today it is unthinkable to talk about gastronomy without referring to its bible, the *Michelin Guide*, which awards annual stars to the best establishments, and it is the absolute reference of its kind.

The book was created by the Michelin brothers, co-founders of the company that bears their name, for the 1900 Universal Exhibition. It was then an advertising guide offered for the purchase of tires.

It was only thirty years later that the one, two, and three star classification appeared in the book to reward restaurants "on the road to the sun"—the Paris-Lyon-Marseille axis on the national roads 6 and 7.

The goal was, of course, to make people "consume tires" to discover these good restaurants.

I recall that the stars of the guide distinguish establishments of all styles, offering the best quality of cuisine. The criteria are (according to the guide): the choice of products, creativity, the mastery of cooking and flavors, the quality/price ratio, and regularity.

I would like to mention two interesting clarifications about the *Michelin*. First, the term *macaron*, frequently used instead of *star*, comes from a journalist who incorrectly used this word in an article to avoid repetition. However, only the term *star* is officially recognized by the book.

The *Michelin Guide* is commonly called the *Red Guide*, in reference to the color of its cover. Its creators chose red to differentiate it from green, the color of another tourist guide published by the same company.

We've been hearing the refrain for years: France no longer has a monopoly on the best culinary establishments. So many restaurants, from Shanghai to Berlin, and from Barcelona to London, compete every year for the honorary title of "best table in the world." Less and less often, France manages to place one of its restaurants on the top of the ranking. But the French can still claim to keep a certain control, remaining the supreme judges... through their gastronomic bible!

The eternal competitor of Michelin, the Italian Pirelli, also became famous for an activity entirely opposite to the tire manufacturing. Every year, the company publishes a calendar featuring young women so scantily clad...
It's very strange to see that those companies are mostly popular thanks to publications far away from their core business!

A good meal ends with a small sweet——the dessert. And before this, there is another food of which the French are world champions in all categories: cheese.
It is even said that cheese was the first food shaped by the hand of man.
According to legend, our ancestors produced the first cheese completely by accident. In the distant past, milk

was transported in skins made from mammalian stomachs. However, when placed into contact with rennet (an enzyme naturally present in the stomach of ruminants), the milk would have produced curds and whey. This was the birth of cheese as we know it.

The Gallic lands produce more than a thousand different cheeses. Between the AOC, the AOP, the hard, the soft, and the marbled, it is difficult to find one's way if one is not a scholar.

Nevertheless, I will try to provide a simplified description.

Traditionally, French cheeses are divided into eight families. They are all made from one of the three sources of animal milk: cow's, goat's, or sheep's milk.

If eight categories prove too difficult to handle, Gallic cheese can just as easily be classified into three dominant groups: the hard, the soft and the blue, and that's much more easy to understand, especially to our palates...

About forty cheeses are AOC (*Appellation d'origine contrôlée*), about thirty have the AOP (*Appellation d'origine protégée*, also known as PDO), and about fifty have the privilege to have both appellations. The AOC is a French system designed to guarantee adherence to strict production methods, specific to a particular field . And the AOP (PDO) is the counterpart of the AOC, but issued by the European Union.

For cheese, we also use the word *terroir* to refer to the geographic area in which it is produced, and France has more than twenty cheese regions. This is how we find in our plates *brousse, brie, camembert, munster, livarot, cantal, laguiole, gruyère, comté, reblochon, tome, rocamadour,* crotin de Chavignol, roquefort, *Bleu de Bresse,* and *Boursin,* among others.

It is interesting to note that in France, cheese was frequently made in monasteries, a bit like the monks who brewed beer in Belgium. It is therefore no coincidence that most of the great French cheeses are derived from old monastic recipes, such as *Pont-l'évêque, Munster, Maroilles,* or the *tête de moine.*

Holland is a strong competitor to France for its cheese, mainly thanks to its *gouda* and *edam.* This rivalry has inspired advertisers to refer to the Netherlands as "the other country of cheese," but above all, to avoid offending anyone in France!

Charles de Gaulle once made the mythical statement: "How do you want to govern a country where there are two hundred and fifty-eight varieties of cheese?"

Today, there are much more than one thousand varieties of cheese, so governing France should be even more complicated!

And what do you eat cheese with? Bread, of course! And here is another Gallic specialty, which has also become a physical stereotype: the French and their baguette of bread under the arm.

A president has even taken steps to have the French baguette given UNESCO World Heritage status, a magnificent distinction in prospect for this piece of bread, barely eighty centimeters long, renowned for its crunchiness and soft interior.

Annually, France produces a whopping six billion baguettes, so the stereotype is hardly overused...

Gastronomy has inspired many writers in ancient Gaul, and this has certainly helped its worldwide fame. One goes so far as to mention the term *gourmet literature*!

Brillat-Savarin (1755-1826), in his book *Physiology of Taste*, was the first to underline the links between gastronomy, physics, chemistry, and political economy.

Alexandre Dumas was said to be an excellent amateur cook. He devoted the end of his life to the writing of the *Grand dictionnaire de cuisine*, a work containing more than three thousand recipes.

And obviously there are the satirical novels of François Rabelais, with its protagonists the greedy giants Gargantua and Pantagruel, fathers of the expressions *pantagruelic* and *gargantua*n.

The French film industry has not been left out of the phenomenon. *La Grande Bouffe, L'Aile ou la Cuisse, Le Grand Restaurant,* and more recently, *Vatel*, the story of a chef with a tragic destiny, played by Gérard Depardieu at the height of his powers, are just some examples.

Curiously, gastronomy is also deliciously present in the insults of the language of Molière.

A quiche is not only a salty dish with smoked bacon, but also a slang term for someone who is a bit clumsy and awkward.

Tarte is not only used for a culinary dish, but it also refers to a person who has not acted with "great intelligence."

Primarily a pastry, a flan is also an adjective that can also be used to refer to an individual who is not considered to be very dynamic.

François Hollande was given the nickname Flanby by his detractors owing to his supposedly soft and indecisive character. But the former president, also known and appreciated for his sense of humor, once said, "They want to hurt me, but it is a very good proposal: I do not know anyone who does not like Flanby!"

Fruits and vegetables are equally present in this field.

A good pear (*poire*) is used for someone who is easily fooled.

The word *truffle* is commonly used for someone who is gullible and stupid, as well as a squash or a dummy.

On the other hand, "*avoir la banane*" (having the banana) is an allegory that refers to the shape of the banana and the shape of our mouth when we are happy and smiling.

The expression "*avoir la patate*" (literally, "to have the potato") has an identical meaning and refers to the head shape. When we have "la patate," we have a good head, or at least that's what we say...

The expression has also evolved over time to become "*avoir la frite*" (to have the fries). However, for this last expression, there is no longer any reference to the head shape. If this were the case, one might be a little concerned...

In the phrase "I've got a big potato" (*j'en ai gros sur la patate*), the word potato means *heart*; therefore, to have a big weight on the heart means that you are sad and unhappy.

The word potato is definitely used in all sorts of ways, since we also say "to pass the potato" (*se refiler la patate chaude*) to get rid of someone or something annoying.

Continuing with the theme of vegetables commonly used in the French language menu, we also say "c'est un navet" (it's a turnip) to describe a mediocre film. If you don't have any money, the expression *"je n'ai pas un radis"* (I don't even have a radish) is often used. To describe the physique of a tall person with a thin build, some people use the term asparagus.

We also find the weight of gastronomy in countless Gallic expressions, such as *met les petits plats dans les grands* (literally, "putting the small plats into the big ones"), meaning that someone will host you with magnificence. And if he has *un cœur d'artichaut* (an artichoke heart), he will easily fall in with you. If he *met du beurre dans les épinards* (to put butter in the spinach), he will soften his bad mood. But if *il raconte des salades* (he tells salads), then he won't tell you the truth. If he has *pain sur la planche* (bread on the table) in other work, then he has a lot of work. And If somebody *tombe dans les pommes* (falls into the apples), meaning to faint, maybe it's just because he is tired of *faire le poireau* (to make the leak) waiting for too long. So, let's hope the situation won't *tourner au vinaigre* (turn sour) getting worse. In any case, *on ne va pas en faire un fromage* (we won't make a cheese out of it), for this is not such a big deal.

French is definitely a language to be savored!

And gastronomy is so present in French society that it has become an obsession.

We also recognize the considerable influence of French cuisine with the many expressions of French origin used in foreign languages: chef, croissant, baguette, champagne, vinaigrette, à la carte, amuse-bouche, apéritif, brioche, crème brûlée, entremets, mousse, digestif, bon vivant, and of course, bon appétit!

To finish this chapter, here are two anecdotes about my family-in-law, illustrating embarrassing situations generated by the inappropriate use of Victor Hugo's language, but linked to food...

My late father-in-law had made a friend during his studies in Paris, named Carlos, of Argentine origin. Carlos came from a wealthy family, and to celebrate the end of their studies, the Argentine invited his Spanish-speaking friend to a starred restaurant in the French capital, *La Tour d'Argent*.

When the waiter approached the two young guests to ask them if they had enjoyed the meal, Carlos' answer was clear:

"*C'était pas dégueulasse*" (it was not disgusting).

A curious and insolent answer, to say the least, pronounced by a young man barely 20 years old after having tasted a meal accessible to so few.

But the guest in question was not French, and that is important. In the mouth of a compatriot, such a remark is completely incorrect, whether in a starred restaurant or in any other table. So, let's admit that the impertinence of the sentence is due to a misuse of Voltaire's language.

But in any case, what has happened to Carlos to cause him to use the word *disgusting* in such circumstances?

According to my father-in-law, the facial expression of the waiter after his friend's answer was worth the delicious meal.

And the line went down in our family, crossing generations... and almost certainly in the waiter's family, too!

My brother-in-law Iñaki, despite being Spanish, is also very fluent in French. However, it is difficult to express oneself in a foreign language without a "foreign" accent, and Iñaki is no exception to the rule.

While we were sitting at a restaurant on the Basque coast, the waiter and I heard the following sentence in his voice:

"As a main course, I'm going to have a magret de connard. (*Cannard* is a duck, but *connard* is an asshole. You just change one letter and the meaning changes completely).

Most people are left astonished whenever this last word is pronounced.

"A margret of... what?" asked the waiter.

"De *connard*," insisted my brother-in-law.

Or at least, that's what we heard again, with his lovely Spanish accent.

The waiter left with his order with a huge smile on his face. I'm sure he was quick to tell his friends and family about this delightful anecdote, laughing heartily at the situation.

As for us, needless to say that with such an introduction, this family meal was extremely joyful.

The dish in question, tastefully matched with figs

United colors of France:
a very colorful country

While sitting at a bar in a little village in southern Italy, watching an exciting World Cup match between France and the Netherlands, my neighbor, who either didn't know much about soccer or was a little tipsy from the double Martini he had just had, asked me which African team was playing against the Dutch.

At every sporting event, we hear the same story again and again. France, with its large contingent of players coming from ethnic minorities (mostly African and Caribbean), is mocked.

When I say that I was born in Marseille, the comment "but there are a lot of Arabs in Marseille" comes along the conversation sooner or later, depending on the degree of proximity of my interlocutor.

But this is the real face of France today—a multiracial, multireligious, multicultural, multicolored country—and we should be proud of it!

Even so, this is not so simple...

The typical Frenchman at the dawn of the third millennium is undoubtedly darker-skinned, browner-haired, and less light-eyed than he was a century ago.

A fact that cannot be denied, the South runs into the veins of many French people.

Searching for the origin of this melting pot is relatively basic and easy. It is enough to go back to the time of the colonies.

France and the United Kingdom have built the two largest colonial empires on our world. From the Pacific to Antarctica, through America and, of course, Africa, the colonists from France left an indelible mark on the lands where they settled.

Culture, language, religion, and education were inculcated with equal devotion in Paris, Dakar, or Guyana.

The story of the African schoolboy learning in history class about "his ancestors the Gauls" is not a joke. This type of situation really happened because the textbooks were not adapted to the place where they were distributed.

Nevertheless, unlike other colonial powers such as Portugal, Spain, and the United Kingdom, France still has a very large number of overseas territories today.

The tricolor flag can be seen not only in Europe, but also in the middle of the Pacific, the Indian Ocean, the Caribbean, America and the South Pole.

No nation in the whole world can rival France in the extent and diversity of its territories.

And people have migrated, they have mixed, they have intermingled... and here we are today.

At the time of decolonization, some even chose France as their place of residence rather than their country of birth. Frequently also, because it could not be otherwise...

The harkis, those soldiers who fought for the French army against their Algerian brothers, are touching examples. The word harki is derived from the Arabic word *harka*, which means movement.

And what a movement, what a Cornelian choice!
On the other side of the Mediterranean, the word *harki* has become synonymous with traitor or collaborator.

The Senegalese riflemen (les tirailleurs sénégalais) are another example of obedience to the colonial power. These African soldiers, enlisted by the French army, fought not only in the two world wars, but also in conflicts between France and its own colonies such as in Indochina, Algeria and Madagascar.
What allegiance! But did they have the choice? That's another debate...

After these acts of bravery, how can we not welcome in France, those who have put their lives at risk for her?

Today, the Hexagon has kept strong links with its former colonies, particularly in Africa, due to the proximity of language and culture (naturally, since we have the same Gallic ancestors...), so much so that the expression "Françafrique" is used in this respect.

This pejorative neologism was born from the supposed interference of the Gallic authorities in the internal affairs of its former territories.

As a matter of fact, the former colonial power is sometimes omnipresent...
Militarily, thanks to its permanent bases in Côte d'Ivoire, Djibouti, Senegal, Gabon, Chad, among others. Economically, France remains, for a significant number of African countries, the privileged partner. And politically, without interfering directly as it was the case in the past through "muscular" interventions, the supposedly *big brother protector* is nevertheless watching over.

A little anecdote that will hopefully make you smile.

Eleven French-speaking African states had joined forces to found an airline, which could only be called *Air Afrique*. Air France was one of the main shareholders of the defunct company. It was defunct because a series of negative factors and the rising cost of kerosene grounded the aircraft of this attractive project of continental cooperation.

A friend who used to work for *Air Afrique* told me about an unusual ritual that took place at each traditional Christmas meal at the company's Paris headquarters.

At the time of the distribution of the chocolates, the white workers were required to take only black chocolates and the black employees only white chocolates. And beware of anyone who made this mistake! He was immediately the laughing stock of the entire audience for the rest of the evening.

A very nice humorous symbol, neither tasteless nor colorless!

In France, the expression *black-blanc-beur* (literally) *is* commonly used to refer to the variety of its people. *Black* for the Caribbean and African with roots, *blanc* for white, and *beur* being a colloquial term to designate French from Arab origin.

But the country is not only *black-blanc-beur,* since it has also attracted many other nations, such as the Spanish fleeing the dark years of Francoism. Many French proudly boast of their Italian origins, not to mention the Portuguese, who are the largest foreign community in France, if we exclude the Maghreb countries. Thus, Da

Silva, Lopez, and Esposito naturally rub shoulders with Dupont and Durand in our phone book.

Just by looking at a map we can easily understand why France remains a land of passage, and also of asylum. To the north, south, and east, the Hexagon shares its borders, and is third only to the immense territories of Russia and China as the nation with the most neighbors. No less than eleven countries share borders with ancient Gaul and its overseas possessions.

France is also home to a large community of people who share the Jewish faith. After the United States, and of course, Israel, it is the nation with the most Jews on its soil. For facts and figures, we also add that the largest contingent of Muslims in Europe is in France.
And all this beautiful melting pot must cohabit, coexist, and cooperate, which is not so simple.

Nowadays, a very high proportion of the immigrant population or of immigrant origin lives in the suburbs of the largest French cities. Many of those areas suffer from insecurity, unemployment, and drug dealing. It doesn't take much for an entire neighborhood go kindle, which has unfortunately happened too often in the past. Vaulx-en-Velin in 1990, Nanterre in 1995, Clichy-sous-Bois in 2005, and Aulnay-sous-Bois in 2017 are unfortunate examples of suburbs of big cities (Paris and Lyon) that suffered from violent confrontations between their young citizens and police forces.

One can point out the architectural design of these suburbs, for most of them were built after the Second World War. They are isolated from city centers, underequipped with cultural and sports facilities, and lack a community life. Local businesses flee them after the first acts of vandalism. The youth and the police in these areas are in a permanent state of conflict. And public opinion stigmatizes them...

Did the French suburbs become the ghettos of modern times?

We all hope that this question will never arise.

In this somewhat bleak landscape, there are, however, beautiful stories that give reason for hope.
Many personalities from the French suburbs are magnificent examples of success thanks to their artistic talents, especially in the field of music and comedy. Singers Aya Nakamura, Maître Gims, or comedians Omar Sy are convincing cases, among many others.
A similar observation can be made for sportsmen and women, as sport is a wonderful factor of integration for young people from minorities, notwithstanding my bar neighbor in Italy... We will come back to this later.

The French audiovisual and political landscape is more and more represented by the communities. Some will say that it is not yet sufficiently represented, but when compared to a few decades ago, the statement is obvious.

We can also say that the cohabitation between Jews and Muslims, considering the size of these two communities in France, and except for some isolated cases, has gone rather smoothly.

In any case, to quote the Buddhist monk Matthieu Ricard, "It is too late to be pessimistic!".

One might also wonder whether France is a socially "divided" country.

Although some "mixing" has taken place, observing what happens in my country, with the hindsight of my years of living abroad, I would answer yes to this question.

There are even groups of people in France who are completely atypical, and who could almost be compared to social classes. They are so characteristic that they have few equivalents in other countries of the world.

The "Cathos" are a perfect example.

As its abbreviation indicates, it is a group of people who have in common the Catholic religion, and above all, its assiduous practice. But this is not their only common point. Most Catholics come from noble and middle-class families in France; and for a great number of them, they come from large families.

A funny story about this: a friend of mine had invested in a spacious vehicle (the Renault Espace, to be exact) to transport his very large family. We immediately renamed the car the *cathomobile*, in reference to the *papamobile* of the Holy Father in Rome and the spacious vehicles that large families like.

During the dancing parties, *the cathos* are easily identifiable: they are the only ones dancing rock 'n' roll!

An English friend once specifically asked me about this: "But why do the French know how to rock dance so well? Do they teach it in schools?
My answer was that in France, you don't learn to dance rock 'n' roll in school, but at rallies. And as for this person

(as for so many others) the word rally was immediately associated with a car race. While considering my answer, his face was one of utter astonishment.

"Rally and rock 'n' roll, but what does that have to do with anything?"

A rally is certainly a car race, but it is also the name given to a certain kind of dance party.

Originally, these parties were organized by mothers who wanted their children to marry people from a similar social, cultural, and religious background. Today, associations, and even commercial companies, have taken over their organization, although their objective remains the same: to promote meetings between individuals with certain "common values."

The churches of ancient Gaul are, in our time, entirely taken over by *the Catho*. Not so long ago, one could still find at Sunday mass a social mix perfectly representative of French families, from the most destitute to the most well-to-do. However, this is less and less the case...

Today in France, the *Catho* holds the flame of the Catholic religion at arm's length, and against all odds, in a country that is frequently described as *the eldest daughter of the Church* (because king Vercingetorix was the first world leader to get catholic religion).

The bourgeois-bohemian (aka *bobo*) represents another social category that warrants special attention.

To draw a portrait of the *bobo*, one could say that it is a person with a rather well-to-do income, with higher education and strong ideological and social convictions.

The singer Renaud (himself acknowledging that he was one of them) specially dedicated a song to them, of which here are some extracts:

"They are a bit of an artist, that's something,
But their passion is their job.
In the computer industry or in the media,
They are proud to pay a lot of taxes...
They smoke a joint from time to time,
They shop in organic markets,
Drive a 4x4, but most of the time,
Prefer to travel by bike...
They like Japanese restaurants and Korean movies,
Spend their vacations in the French Riviera...
They like Jack Lang and Sarkozy,
But they always vote for ecologists."

Whatever the definition we can give, the *bobo* is quite representative of the French people and their state of mind. An individual who has difficulties to choose between his well-being and his conscience, his wallet and his morals value. But without ever really making a decision in favor of one or the other. He is a hybrid! The French made the Revolution cut the head of their king and then adore an equally undemocratic emperor. In the midst of the post-Thirty Glorious capitalist euphoria, they elected a left-wing president. A few years later, during the cohabitation, they opted for a prime minister with political ideas entirely opposed to those of their president.

There are so many examples in ancient Gaul of this duality of choice and consciousness, and the *bobo*, coming back to him, is wonderfully representative of this mindset.

Do you know that France is the first European agricultural power, and the second world exporter of agricultural products, just after the United States? You might ask yourself: what does this have to do with social classes?

Well, because the peasantry is considered in France as a social class in its own right! And the French consider it, without a doubt, the most worshiped and respected class. Those who "work the land" generally benefit from a deep sympathy capital, which they deserve. Not to mention that they feed us!

The Agricultural Merit, an award for services rendered to agriculture, is one of the first honorary orders in a country that has twenty million cows in its pastures and stables!

Then, it is not so surprising to see French TV shows like *L'amour est dans le pré* (love is in the countryside), whose concept is to help single farmers find their soul mate, beating audience records year after year.

Politicians are not mistaken either, courting the farmer like few others, not only in order to collect precious votes, but also to take advantage of his influence on society. Thus, few French presidents have missed the traditional annual meeting at the Paris International Agricultural show.

But despite this, the sector is in crisis. The number of farmers in France continues to decrease. Fifty years ago, there were still three million of them; today, there are barely four hundred thousand. The agricultural surface, which covers half of the territory, is undergoing a similar fate, giving up more and more land in favor to urbanized areas.

In a country where the majority of the active population works thirty-five hours a week and enjoys many weeks of paid leave, the harsh living conditions of the farmer do not make the new generations fantasize.

Young people dream of start-ups, social networks, and city life... not so much about combines, cornfields, or tractors.

Your humble narrator comes from a farming family. My mother is actually decorated with the *poireau* (leek), a colloquial nickname given to the Agricultural Merit. I was lucky enough to spend my childhood playing between bales of hay and running through beautiful meadows. In a shed, we had a tractor from the prestigious Porsche brand, at a time when the German manufacturer was still making industrial vehicles.

At school, I regularly bragged about having a "Porsche" at home. When my friends came to visit me in the farmhouse where we lived, I enjoyed so much watching their faces at the sight of the Porsche in question...

In this chapter, we have gone from the suburbs to the rally parties, from the soccer player of African descent to the *bobos* of the upper-class neighborhoods and to the peasant of our fields.
But this is all about what France is today. A mixed country, diverse and colorful: a united colors country!

Yes, indeed, Porsche did build tractors, and even diesel models!

The glass half full... of wine

It is impossible to write a book about the French without mentioning their favorite drink, the one that joins most of their meals and contributes to the reputation of their know-how all over the world.

We can't deny the fact that the ménage à trois of food, wine, and France, go hand in hand.

Between the section on cooking and this one, dedicated to wine, I have nevertheless added another chapter, in order to avoid that this book becomes a gastronomic and oenological guide!

I recently overheard a person (French, I may not need to add) who, referring to the famous expression: "I prefer to say that the glass is half full rather than half empty," added the words "of wine" just after the word glass, with the blessing of his interlocutor. That is, without the interlocutor (also French), pointing out to him that this addition was absolutely fortuitous... or not.

Anyway, in France, the glass of wine is more often empty than full!

The divine nectar as we call it, is undeniably an ancestral Gallic custom, just like tea for the English, whisky for the Scots, and beer for the Germans and Belgians.

Like gastronomy, it represents an essential component of the French way of life and one of the best ambassadors of the country.

The figures speak for themselves: three quarters of French people admit to drinking at least one glass of wine every day!

And to justify its consumption, its therapeutic benefits are overexposed.

Red wine, thanks to the polyphenols it contains, has antioxidant virtues, a key element for heart and cholesterol problems. Consequently, the risk of stroke would be clearly reduced thanks to its consumption.

Further, medical research has demonstrated that wine consumption is beneficial for patients suffering from digestive cancer or lung cancer. And to preserve and improve eyesight, the divine nectar is recommended to fight age-related degeneration. Wine also reduces the risk of depression thanks to the magical effect of resveratrols.

So what does this word, so difficult to pronounce, refer to?

Resveratrols are organic molecules, present in grapes skin, that the vine produces to defend itself from fungi. Once in our body, those "magic" resveratrols act by forming a protection on certain areas of our brain.

For example, resveratrols limit weight gain by naturally reducing appetite and preventing the body from storing fat cells.

Americans speak of the "French paradox": how can the French eat so much animal fat and have such a low heart attack rate?

So, after this paragraph worthy of a medical prescription, are you convinced of the wine virtues?

In any case, these are excellent excuses to drink it!

But if wine is the most natural and beneficial alcoholic beverage for health, let's not forget that it is also the first cause of alcoholism in France.

More than one generation of French people still have in mind the advertising slogans that have become mythical: "Did you see yourself when you drank?" (*Tu t'es vu quand t'as bu?*) or "One glass is fine ; three glasses, hello the damage" (*un verre, ça va, trois verres, bonjour les dégâts*).

Although some of the wine properties are beneficial to humans, it has also demonstrated that excessive consumption (as with other alcoholic beverages) considerably reduces life expectancy.

Politicians have inevitably had to take these facts into account.

A Minister of Health, the aptly named Claude Évin, drafted a law in 1991 that was intended to regulate the advertising of alcoholic beverages, but did not ban it. It is from this law that we could read on alcohol advertisements messages evoking the dangers of its abuse.

But the text has been amended many times, for more flexibility, probably under the pressure of powerful lobbies. This is somewhat of a global paradox, because the trend is more to a hardening of the laws on alcohol consumption, rather than to a softening...

Just like with art, here comes another example of French exception!

One might think that the Frenchies are the world's leading wine producers, but think again, it is the Italians, and soon the Spanish, who are ahead of us in this field.

France can nevertheless console itself by consulting its export statistics, the French nectar being by far the most consumed wine abroad. Spirits even rank second among the products exported from the old Gaul, just after Airbus planes, but before perfumes and cosmetics. This is not surprising for a sector so generous in terms of employment in order to provide human resources for the eighty thousand or so wine-producing farms of the country.

All initiatives are welcome to promote the fruit of the vine. The media slaughter created each year for the launching of the *Beaujolais Nouveau*, on the third Thursday of November, is one of the most spectacular demonstrations of this.

All means are also good to sell the production, because France remains a land blessed by the gods for the culture of the vine.

The Hexagon hosts on its soil no less than seventeen wine-producing regions. From Alsace to Corsica, through Roussillon, Burgundy, Lyonnais, Jura, Languedoc, and many others. Only the Channel coast and the North of France do not produce wine.

For instance, the Bordeaux region has no less than sixty AOC appellations. But contrary to what one might think, it is not the first French wine region, since the Languedoc, with its three hundred thousand hectares of vines, takes the lead.

For the wines of Bordeaux, we speak of "premier grand cru classé" for the five most prestigious of them: château Lafite Rothschild, château Mouton Rothschild, château Latour, château Margaux, château Haut-Brion.

But there are also second, third, fourth and fifth Cru.

The first classification took place in 1855 at the request of Napoleon III, for the Universal Exhibition of Paris, with the aim of differentiating the wines exhibited, such as magnificent standards of French know-how.

One might also wonder why so many Gallic wines contain the word *château*.

An 1857 law, written to protect trademarks, stipulated the need to add a distinctive character to the historical identification of the wines. Thus, the words *domaine*, *château*, *clos*, *mas*, *abbaye*, etc., began to be used.

At a time when almost every farmer cultivated a few vines, the wealthiest farmers took advantage of this opportunity to distinguish themselves by adding the word château to the name of their vineyard.

In France, most people raise their glasses filled with red wine, however, little by little, rosé is gaining ground.

For a long time, rosé has been considered as a by-product, causing a terrible hangover, and only consumed in summer. This image has changed up to the point of becoming the type of wine with the most exponential growth in recent years. Its production has even surpassed that of white wine.

Americans, among others, love rosé and are the second largest consumers in the world.

Rosé is the "cool" wine, the one that establishes a connivance, the one that we usually drink when we are on vacation.

We can afford to mix it. Rosé-grapefruit is a great success and, more surprisingly, other drinks such as pastis and beer are also being mixed with rosé!

Just like gastronomy, French wine know-how is not immune to stiff competition. But there is one area in the country that resists all forms of usurpation without the slightest fear. The name of its wine is the homonym of its region. It is, as you may have guessed it, champagne.

Just like the Eiffel Tower or the Arc de Triomphe, this sparkling alcoholic drink is one of the most prestigious symbols of the country.

It will never be rivaled, at least in name, because only wines produced, harvested, and elaborated in the delimited area "Champagne in France" can be called "champagne," a territorial parcel defined by a law extending over thirty-four thousand hectares.

Champagne is the only French wine that can be made by mixing red and white wine. It is produced according to a rigorous method, called *champenoise*.

According to the popular belief, this method was invented by Dom Pérignon, a monk from a local abbey. A prestigious brand of sparkling wine bears his name.

On report of a study, a champagne cork can reach 40 km/h when expelled, because of the pressure contained in the bottle.

And once again, I have a very true anecdote to tell you about this.

During the engagement of one of my uncles, his brother (another uncle) was in charge of the aperitif, uncorking one by one the magnums of Veuve Clicquot marvelously commandeered for the occasion.

But a rebellious cork escaped his attention, and particularly that of his fingers, to go and lodge itself with power and determination, after a very short flight... in the eye of the bride's mother.

The poor woman was briefly left with a black eye that had tripled in size, the perfect boxer's black eye.

We almost reached a diplomatic incident with this somewhat traumatized mother-in-law, and all because of a champagne cork. Fortunately, the woman inflicted more fear than harm, since the incident had no medium-term consequences for the mother-in-law's ocular capacities.

This evening could not have been more sparkling to say the least.

Since that event, every time an uncle of my family opens a bottle, whatever the vintage, the audience, cautiously advised, dives instantly under the table.

According to some historical hypotheses, the first balls used in table tennis were champagne corks. I think that my uncle's mother-in-law would have preferred to receive a ping-pong ball in her eye rather than this cursed cork projectile...

France is not only famous for its wine, be it red, rosé, white, or sparkling. Among the other alcoholic beverages produced in France, two stand out for their international

99

reputation: Armagnac and Cognac. They are the most famous brandy.

Cognac is said to have been created by winegrowers who wanted to export their low-alcohol white wine to England and Holland. They had the idea of distilling it to better export it and to add water to it once at destination. The result was a white brandy of bad quality. But the producers discovered that the longer the wine remained in the barrel, the more the liquid was transformed into a delicious liqueur. Thus, cognac, was born.

It was an immediate success in Holland, to such an extent that the winegrowers produced it exclusively for the Dutch market. They called it *brandewijn*, meaning burnt wine, from which the word "brandy" was derived.

Armagnac has long been considered the "poor little brother" of cognac. And yet, it is much older. According to some historians, it was created in the middle of the 13th century as a very popular therapeutic remedy, specifically used to soothe nerves!

Only three hundred kilometers apart, cognac is widely consumed more than its neighbor at a rate of thirty-five bottles against only one for armagnac. But according to connoisseurs, only Armagnac is capable of fully satisfying fine palates.

As a curious phenomenon, over the past few decades, cognac has become the favorite drink of American rappers! They don't hesitate to show off on social networks branding bottles brandy, and go as far as quoting brands in their songs.

It goes without saying, the publicity delights the French producers, even if these urban music artists are not really a target audience they would have thought of at first.

While in most countries, alcoholic beverages of more than forty degrees are enjoyed as digestives, France stands out once again, sometimes consuming them... as aperitifs!
And among the famous French aperitifs, one deserves special attention thanks to its popularity. This is *pastis*.
Paradoxically, this beverage was created because of a ban on drinks with too much alcohol!
The 19th century was marked by the frenetic consumption of absinthe, an alcoholic drink that supposedly drove people mad. In 1915, a decree forbade any drink containing more than 16 degrees of alcohol.
But the French were not of this opinion, given their love of consuming aniseed drinks mixed with water (absinthe is elaborated with green anise). So, in 1920, the government had to backtrack, allowing aniseed drinks up to thirty degrees of alcohol. Then, in 1922, the number of degrees was raised to forty.
A man named Paul Ricard, son of a wine merchant, spent many hours in his makeshift laboratory testing various combinations to create a recipe that included star anise, green anise and licorice.
He named his invention *pastis*, a word derived from the Provençal *pastisson* and the Italian *pasticchio* meaning mixture. It was an immediate success. Today, the *petit jaune* (the little yellow) as we call it, is an icon of the French aperitif.

In addition to wine, champagne, cognac, armagnac, and pastis, the regions of ancient Gaul have abounded in resources to produce a considerable number of aperitifs and digestifs. Calvados, chartreuse, rum (ti-punch), kirsch, floc de Gascogne, Benedictine are magnificent examples of drinks that pleasure our taste buds.

Cheers!

By the way, in France when we toast, not only do we say *santé* (health), but also *tchin-tchin*. These expressions both have their origins in the Middle Ages (like so many others), a splendid period of French history when it was not unusual to "unintentionally" pour a few drops of poison into the cup of one's enemy. In order to ensure that one's drink was not dangerously lethal, exchanging a little of one's drink with one's neighbors was, therefore, a widely practiced custom. Thus, one would clash one's glass filled to the brim against another's in order to spill a little liquid into each cup. And it is the sound of this noisy contact that would have inspired the onomatopoeia: tchin-tchin.

However, there is another hypothesis. The expression would come from the Chinese *qing qing*, which is pronounced "tchin-tchin," meaning "please." At the time of Napoleon III, the soldiers who campaigned in China for the Emperor explained that the Chinese drank by exchanging "tchin-tchin."

Wines and spirits are also nicely present in many French expressions. We say, "We're not going to make a pastis of it" to play down a situation, especially in the south of France.

"C'est champagne" is an exclamation to evoke something like the drink: unusual and spectacular.

Il faut mettre de l'eau dans son vin (to put some water in his wine), although the French don't like to do it very much, is a locution meaning to soften, to be more moderate.

The expression *verser un pot-de-vin* (pourer un pot-de-vin) is certainly the most common that mentions the famous drink. It refers to the fact of paying a sum of money in an illegal way, with the aim to benefit from an advantage on his part.

And to close this watery chapter, another anecdote, absolutely true once again, illustrating the love of the French for the fruit of the vine.

Uncles and aunts have produced wine in Burgundy for generations. They are also related to our beloved champagne-opening specialist. A few years ago, a mysterious bacterium introduced into the water table dangerously contaminated all the water of this region, where they live. The whole neighborhood suffered from terrible stomach aches. Everyone was sick expect... my uncles and aunts. Doctors and specialists could not explain at first why people were becoming ill en masse but not them.

However, there was a limpid and clear explanation as to why—rock water. This became apparent after an elementary question was put to my relatives: "By the way, when was the last time you drank a glass of water?"

Beautiful flight of a champagne cork.
But be careful with your eyes...

A nation of rebels, with or without a cause

My initial intention was to describe the History of France in a synthetic and humorous way in just a few pages. And then, as the pages went by, I realized that what I had written was neither funny, nor synthetic, and worse, uninteresting!

On top of that, there are so many manuals and books speaking wonderfully of the most important dates of the Gallic people.

This being said, while writing this chapter, one constant came back so frequently that it awakened my attention: the major events of the history of France happened because of the rebellious and insubordinate character of the French.

To use a culinary allegory, we can say that the French are tough cookies. And above all, they hate to be dictated to or told what to do (or not to do).

While not so long ago, many of our neighbors had dictators at their head (Italy, Spain, Germany, among others). Such a fact would have been totally impossible in ancient Gaul, but why?

Because, once again, the Frenchies set themselves apart by starting a revolution against their leaders!

It took a lot of guts (some will use another expression much more familiar) to rebel for more than two hundred years ago against an all-powerful monarchy, and without any means.

The people had everything to lose, and so little to gain. But the right to self-determination is stronger than anything else!

Voltaire said it wisely: "I do not agree with what you say, but I will fight until death so that you have the right to say it."

Though the Revolution deeply transformed French society and is considered as the founding act of modern France. We also talk about a glorification of the Revolution of 1789, because its impact on the current society, more than 230 years later, is still very active.

First of all, thanks to the 1789 events, we have the *Declaration of the Rights of Man and of the Citizen*, and its famous first article: "Men are born and remain free and equal in rights."

This is the basic text of the French Constitution. It was inspired by the United States Declaration of Independence of 1776 and the philosophical spirit of the 18th century.

The motto of the French Republic: "Liberty, Equality, Fraternity," proudly displayed anywhere in public representation of the country, is a product of the Revolution. Although it is additionally a legacy of the century of Enlightenment.

The anthem of *La Marseillaise* is also a tribute to the French Revolution.

One may wonder about the origin of this name, associated with the second largest city of France.

In the beginning, it was called *"Chant de guerre pour l'armée du Rhin"* (war song for the army of Rhine*).* The song was written in Strasbourg by a poet from the Jura during a conflict against Austria.
The poet Claude Joseph Rouget de Lisle composed this war song during the night of April 25 to 26, 1792.
So far, we are really far away from the Mediterranean and the cicadas!
The National Guard of Marseilles would have heard the refrain and recovered it under the name of *Chant de guerre des armées aux frontiers (War song of the armies on the borders).*
In August 1792, when the revolt against the constitutional monarchy broke out in Paris, king Louis XVI was installed in the Tuileries Palace and the Marseillais came to support the revolutionaries by singing the hymn.
With the Tuileries taken and royalty abolished, for the Parisians, this song could only be that of the Marseillais, who had come to put an end to the monarchy.
It was then renamed *La Marseillaise*, in homage to the revolutionaries who had made such a long journey to transform the destiny of their nation.

One line of *La Marseillaise* keeps on dividing opinion: *"qu'un sang impur abreuve nos sillons"* (may impure blood water our furrows).

Some are choked by those words, which could be found appalling, racist, xenophobic, and above all, from another time, for a hymn that is still in force.

But others, including a few historians, refute this thesis, arguing that the verse is misinterpreted, since this "impure blood" is not that of the enemy, but of the revolutionaries! At that time, the plasma of kings and nobles was called pure (or blue) blood.

Still, according to these historians, the verb "to water" should be understood as "nourishing" and the words "our furrows" express the belonging to "our" lands—those we cultivate.

Consequently, with this other reading, Rouget de Lisle would have used irony to say to the nobles: "You will see how our blood, supposedly impure, will be poured (and sacrificed) to nourish our land.

It is also thanks to the French Revolution that we owe the colors of the flag. Blue and red representing the colors of the Parisian revolutionaries (and the city of Paris), framing the white, the color of the king. The flag thus perfectly symbolizes the hold of the people over royalty.

For the other little story, the Gallic flag has vertical stripes in order to differentiate itself from the Dutch flag already in existence at the time, and bearing the same colors, but arranged horizontally.

Marianne was not only a character painted by Eugène Delacroix (cf. painting at the end of this chapter). She was a symbolic muse of the Revolution. More than two centuries later, her bust still holds a place of honor in the town halls and official buildings of the Republic, and her profile appears immutably on French government documents such as stamps and letterheads.

It is interesting to know that her name comes from the contraction of the two first names: Marie and Anne, which were extremely common in the 18th century in popular circles, particularly in the countryside, or among the domestic staff of bourgeois houses.

The red Phrygian cap that Marianne wears on her representations is a reference to the one worn by the freed slaves of ancient Rome. A strong symbol of slaves breaking their chains and becoming free citizens.

Earlier, I mentioned the importance of the baguette in the life of the Gauls.

We have it thanks to the French Revolution!

In the wake of the Rights of Man and Citizen, a decree stipulated that all French people had to eat the same bread—"the bread of equality."

Thus began the standardization of the dimensions of bread, and it was the birth of the baguette.

The French get married without going to church and usually divorce afterwards, if they wish, since a law was enacted in 1792—in the middle of the Revolution. Divorce had finally been abrogated under the Restoration, only to be authorized again some time later.

The Jews of France became full citizens, thanks to a decree passed during the Revolution.

No country had ever achieved such an advance for this sometimes oppressed community. Thus, the French dream entered the hearts of the Jews, as proclaimed by a Yiddish saying: "happy as God in France."

Under the Old Regime, the use of *tutoiement* (informal familiarity) was considered a rude impertinence. A convention of the Revolution made it compulsory, both in the civil and in the administration, in order to express a link of universal fraternity. The application of this convention lasted a short time; nevertheless, what an advance!

It is understandable that the French national holiday, celebrated every July 14, commemorates its revolution, so much so that it marked the history of the country.

It was a bloody period, let us not forget, but so inventive, avant-gardist, and intrepid. The culmination of a century marked by lights.

And at the source of these lights, we find men of letters, who characterize so much the critical and anticonformist spirit of the Frenchies: philosophers, obviously!

When Montesquieu advocates the separation of powers, Bayle criticizes the idolatry of the people towards a god or a king and Voltaire praises the freedom of thought and tolerance, inevitably ideology makes its way into the minds of the crowd.

What if they were right? What if it were true?

Philosophers who dreamed of a world without slavery, without torture, without cruel punishments, where man would be free to determine by himself his way of life and to choose his future.
With enlightened citizens who do not need a monarch or any other figure to think and deliberate. Substituting reason wherever possible: in the face of blind faith, superstition, autocratic regimes, primitive instincts, uncontrolled feelings.

Advocating religious tolerance, including the freedom not to believe in God.

And all this almost three hundred years ago.

What have we done with these beautiful ideologies?

We must admit that we had an Enlightenment, but unfortunately someone extinguished it...

In the twentieth century, ancient Gaul did not experience the inner turmoil of a civil conflict, such as former Yugoslavia or Spain, yet it suffered just as much in its flesh, being one of the main protagonists of the two world wars.

During the second conflict, it once again distinguished itself by its rebellious and unsubmissive character, by going into the "Resistance."

Intelligence, counter-espionage, sabotage, clandestine press, fabrication of false papers, distribution of tracts, rescue of prisoners, all means were good ways of fighting "in one's own way" against the occupying troops, and sometimes against one's own regime (Vichy one).

The French Resistance managed to do what no one had managed before (and even after): to bring together communists, socialists, ecclesiastics, anarchists, Trotskyites, aristocrats, proletarians, monarchists, and even fascists!

Men and women with such diverse profiles and origins were all united for a common cause. Refusing submission and injustice, they put their own lives at risk to save others.

Any resemblance with real facts and persons having existed (between 1789 and 1804, for example) would be only pure and fortuitous coincidence...

The Resistance remains another light in French History that took place in one of its darkest periods.

Unusual anecdotes from that time: every Resistance member had one or more pseudonyms, known only to his comrades in the struggle, in order to confuse the occupying forces. Thus, Jean Moulin, first called Rex, then changed to Max. Some were inspired by Parisian subway stations: Passy, Corvisart, Saint-Jacques, or other famous people: Sultan, Archduke.

The members of the Alliance network called themselves by animal names, which led the Germans to nickname this organization *Noah's Ark*!

After the war, many Resistance fighters kept their pseudonyms or added them to their real names.

The short story *Le Silence de la mer* (the silence of the sea) is a wonderful depiction of a particular way of resisting. It tells the story of a French-speaking German officer, totally in love with French culture, occupying a requisitioned family home. Every evening, during long monologues, the officer preaches the rapprochement of peoples and fraternity. In response, the inhabitants of the house, a man and his niece, impose on him a heavy and tough silence as the ultimate form of resistance, the silence of the sea.

The story, inspired by real events, was published clandestinely during the war. Its author, Jean Bruller, also an early Resistance fighter, took the pseudonym of

Vercors, in reference to the mountain of the same name, where he had been mobilized at the beginning of the conflict.

I am still from a generation whose parents were affected by the World War. My maternal grandparents got married in 1939, my grandfather was immediately taken prisoner, and he did not know his daughter (my mother) until after the armistice was signed, five years after her birth.
The family house located near Avignon was requisitioned for a time. My grandmother told me that at night she used to open the water valves in the cellar where the occupying soldiers slept. Every morning, they complained to their staff about strange water leaks that had occurred during the night... Another way to resist!

Only a few decades after this sad conflict that set the planet ablaze, when everything was going pretty well, in a world that wasn't so bad, our indomitable Frenchies distinguished themselves again, inventing a new revolution.

This one lasted only a month, yet we still talk about it fifty years later—May 68.

I insist on the period and the context of this popular uprising. We are talking about a decade of unparalleled prosperity, the height of the famous "glorious thirty years," when you could quit your job in the morning and find another one in the afternoon.
A happy France with little unemployment, strong economic growth, and notable improvements in living conditions at all levels.

While others were spending their energy sending rockets into space, walking on the moon, or rebuilding their country damaged by war or internal conflict, what were the French doing in their country?

A new revolution!

Among the Gauls, the spirit of rebellion is instinctive, it's even genetic! They just can't help it.
This time, it was the new generation, the post-war baby boomers, the students, who were taking to the streets.
What were they complaining about?
Isms such as capitalism, consumerism, authoritarianism, paternalism, and even American imperialism!
At that time, in terms of authoritarianism, France was not doing badly compared to its neighbors. Spain and Portugal continued to be under the yoke of a dictatorship, and in the East, the communist regimes, so undemocratic, were in full swing...
I will therefore repeat this maxim, which may shock some, but in which I firmly believe: the French live in a paradise when they believe they are in hell!

Naturally, like the Revolution of 1789, May 68 had positive effects on French society, such as the Grenelle "agreements" for workers, university reform for the students, the law on abortion (although it materialized a little later), and more generally, a broad liberalization of morals.
Under the maxim, "it is forbidden to forbid," this month of protest was undoubtedly a catalyst to "break certain locks."
The famous song *69 année érotique (69 erotic year)*, written by Serge Gainsbourg in 1968, would certainly not

have been able to pass between the stitches of the censorship, without such a liberation of manners...

But this month of violent protests also deeply divided the French society.

Influenced or not by the events in France, at such a time, a wind of rebellion blowed on the blue planet. Prague experienced its springtime of protest, Americans took to the streets to denounce the war in Vietnam, which they considered unjustified. And even in docile Japan, a student league started a movement followed by many.

Coincidence or not, 86 is the anagram of 68. It was a year when our young Frenchies once again demonstrated vehemently against a bill to reform French universities. Among other things, this reform planned to introduce a selection process at the entrance of the universities, and to put them in competition. The project was withdrawn in December 1986, but the uprising will remain forever marked by the unfortunate death of a student.

The yellow vest (gilets jaunes) was known until 2018 as a piece of clothing that one kept preciously in the trunk of his car, and intended to be worn only in cases of extreme necessity.
The protest genius of the Frenchman has transformed this ornament into a symbol of rebellion.
The movement started with a call to demonstrate against a prices increase for motor fuels, which resulted in a new tax (TICPE) on energy products.
The uprising has gradually turned into a revolt against government action, through acts of presence on the roads, traffic circles, and demonstrations every Saturday.

The avenue of the Champs-Élysées and the Arc de Triomphe will certainly be remembered for the yellow vests movement, but also the black bloc groups, who took advantage of the whirlwind to sow discord and cause major alterations. Faced with the magnitude of the phenomenon, the government had to withdraw the TICPE tax, but this did not prevent the Yellow Vests from continuing their protest.

It's sometimes hard to understand the obstinance of the Frenchies...

It must also be said that the French are the world champions of strikes. Between 2008 and 2017, the country experienced an average of one hundred and eighteen strike days per year per thousand employees. That's seven times more than our German neighbors! For the same period, the British had only twenty-one strike days and the Americans five...

In December 2019, ancient Gaul once again experienced a deep strike movement affecting all public transport. At the origin of this protest that paralyzed the whole country was a proposed law on retirement that had not yet been presented publicly.

The Gauls, as a consequence, went on strike just in case, if ever, preventively.

Always stronger, always higher!

Of course, I do not want to make any judgments about these facts; they are only observations. The strikers certainly have legitimate reasons to go on strike. I am just observing what is happening in my country, albeit from a distance, since I do not live there anymore.

Should I also remind you that the French word *grève* (strike) comes from the name of a square in Paris, where unemployed workers used to gather to get hired...

What an irony of fate!

After all, it's not so surprising that *Asterix the Gaul* is the favorite comic strip of the French. It perfectly sums up what they love above all else: insubordination, rebellion, resistance, the little David fighting against the mighty Goliath.

Anyway, as General de Gaulle so wisely said, it is so difficult to govern a country that has so many varieties of cheese!

The vision of the painter Eugène Delacroix of
Liberty leading the People during the Revolution.
What a beautiful image of freedom!

The French and work:
I love you, I love you not

The Grand Canyon of the United States is one of the most beautiful wonders that Mother Nature has given to our globe. For millions of years, one river, just one, has carved the sandstone, the limestone, and the shale of this rock.

We can easily stay for hours contemplating this breathtaking landscape, which inevitably reminds us that we are so little in front of the greatness of nature and the strength of the elements.

I was lucky enough to see the Grand Canyon, and I, like so many others, was stunned by the splendor and grandeur of the place; that is, until one individual, obviously from the south of France by the sound of his accent, broke the heavy and beautiful surrounding silence (not from the sea this time), with the following words:

"What a work, what an amazing work, I can't believe it. Such a work!"

He was right. It is indeed the result of a hard work made by the Colorado River to split this rock. But in front of the sumptuousness of the site, to hear the word *work* from a Frenchman from the South triggered in me a most inappropriate laugh, considering the circumstances.

Indeed, in front of the majestic, splendid, immense and unique Grand Canyon (the hyperboles to describe it are not exaggerated), it is the word work that first passed by the head of this compatriot!

Reflecting on the relationship of the French with work is a complex exercise given the paradoxes of this relationship.

As such, the French word for work, *travail*, comes from the Latin *tripalium*, which was an instrument of torture composed of three stakes!

Contrary to what one might think, the French attach great importance to work. Already in the Age of Enlightenment, numerous philosophers emphasized its virtues. For instance, Jean-Jacques Rousseau wrote, "Temperance and work are man's best doctors," while Voltaire stated, "Work keeps away from us three great evils: boredom, vice, and need."

According to a recent survey where the question was to judge the place of work in their life, three quarters of French people questioned answered that it was "very important," much more so than the British and Germans who were also consulted, and up to twice as many as the Finns!

Nicolas Sarkozy was partly elected President thanks to his campaign promises based on the values of work, and his famous slogan: "Work more to earn more."

But this does not mean that the French are ready to spend all their time working...

According to the National Institute of Statistics and Economic Studies (INSEE), since 1975, the working time of the French has decreased by three hundred and fifty hours each year, which corresponds to forty-three working days, a mere two months less work per year!

In 1900, people in France worked almost half their lives. Today, the frenchies spend only ten percent of their time on their jobs; an abysmal gap.

The French were even pioneers in terms of *quality of life*, since they came up with the idea of instituting paid vacations well before anyone else.

And in response to the scourge of unemployment, they opted for the thirty-five hour week. The idea, by a very basic arithmetic calculation, was that eight people working at the rate of thirty-five hours a week were equivalent to seven people working for forty hours.
The measure thus encouraged companies to hire to make up for this "supposed" lack of work task.

In practice, the law had a very limited impact on employment, but not on the organization of work and the quality of life of the French. In a few decades, France has become one of the nations where people have the most free time, which is, in no small part, thanks to the famous reductions in working time (called RTT). But they are also some of the most productive workers, managing to maintain the same level of productivity while working much less!

And that's not all; in addition to a reduction in working hours, France's social model is a worldwide reference.

In France, people retire well before the vast majority of other countries in the world, and every citizen is entitled to it.

Medical care is free for the entire population.

The labor code is largely in favor of the worker, unlike in many other countries.

Unemployment benefits are among the most generous.

At the same time, salaries in France are on a par with those in the best-off countries.

If we add to this picture the recognition of trade unions, the status of the civil service, assistance to the disabled, the minimum wage (SMIC) and the active solidarity income (RSA), we can really speak of a welfare state.

And while preserving its social gains, France has managed to remain efficient and competitive in an increasingly aggressive and competitive context resulting from globalization.

So far, so good...

Comfortably installed in the G7 for decades, France is one of the top five economic powers on the planet.

So, with regards to social benefits, the purported pampering of its citizens and both economic and industrial success: are the French living in a paradise they don't know about?

From the south of Europe, I can tell you that people look at France with admiration, and above all, with envy!

As a matter of fact, France *is* a spoiled country, let's not be afraid to say it.

The assets of its natural physiognomy, with its numerous mountain ranges, its kilometers of beaches, the beauty of its villages and cities, as well as its sites of cultural and leisure (Disneyland among others), make ancient Gaul by far the most visited nation in the world.

The foreign currency earned annually from the tens of millions of tourists who visit France has made tourism one of the strongest pillars of the French economy. And given that France is an attractive place to work, a considerable number of multinationals have also chosen to set up in the country.

In France, one out of five employees is a civil servant. The State is therefore omnipresent through its administrations, which largely contributes to the economic activity of the territory. One can even speak of the "socialization" of the country.

To sum up, services (tourism among others), multinationals and administration represent the three strongest bulwarks of the French economy.

But there are also remarkable examples of personal success in France.

Entrepreneur Bernard Arnault is regularly ranked as one of the world's wealthiest people. His group's galaxy, whose common denominator is luxury, includes prestigious brands such as Louis Vuitton, Christian Dior, Guerlain, Loewe, Givenchy, Bulgari, Chaumet, Hublot. Stores: La Samaritaine, Le Bon Marché, and Sephora. He is also famous for his champagne houses, such as Moët & Chandon and the most consumed cognac in the world—Hennessy!

What a path for a man who, at the beginning of his career, had joined a family business that was the antithesis of luxury, since it specialized in public works!

This is also one of the particularities of France; success is usually achieved within the family, as is the case with the Mulliez siblings. This dynasty from the north of the country has developed its concept of mass retailing in all sectors of consumption. They first started with a supermarket chain (Auchan). Then they created retailing stores for consumer needs, such as:

- Clothing: Kiabi
- Automotive service company: Norauto and Midas
- DIY : Leroy merlin
- Home decoration: Saint-Maclou
- Eating: Flunch and Les 3 Brasseurs
- Household appliances and multimedia: Boulanger

But its most dazzling success is certainly the Decathlon chain of stores, whose sports product distribution concept is thriving from China to Brazil.

And France is full of such success stories. For example, the undisputed world leader in cosmetics is under the tricolored banner. Make-up, hair coloring, skin care, shampoo, the company L'Oréal has elegantly declined its know-how in the beauty sector.

The multinational owes its origins to a young chemist, Eugène Schueller, who, after having volunteered for a hair problem submitted by a hairdresser, patented a dyeing process to cover white hair! Today, the Parisian company has made its heiress, Françoise Bettencourt Meyers, one of the richest women in the world.

The Pinault family, owners of Gucci, Yves Saint Laurent, Balenciaga, Boucheron, Pomellato, and so many other brands, represents a new case of Gallic success in the luxury industry. Just like Bernard Arnault, so often his most formidable competitor, the patriarch François Pinault began his career by taking over a family business of wood trading. This is a far cry from the prestigious auction house Christie's, which also belongs to his empire.

The Ricard brotherhood, known for its eponymous pastis, has become one of the leading merchants of wines and spirits in just a few decades through the absorption and development of beverages that make our gullets happy.

Wherever you are, from the Bic pen in your school kit to the Essilor lenses of your glasses, your Seb deep fryer or your favorite perfume, *made in France* has certainly gone some way with you.

Abroad, we know the heavyweights of the French motor industry, such as Renault, Peugeot, Citroën or Bugatti, its supermarkets Carrefour, its yoghurts Danone, or its banks BNP Paribas and Société générale.
A little more discreetly, companies under the tricolor flag are the world leaders in the production of sailboats, malaria vaccines, cable cars, outdoor advertising, and even bar codes!

Once again, after this pleasant picture, I cannot fail to mention the other side of the coin.

In ancient Gaul, we have a highly ambiguous relationship with money that is singularly different from that of Anglo-Saxon countries, among others.

Asking someone how much he earns is very badly perceived in France, even if he is a friend or family member. It is considered as a lack of education. And showing off your money is even worse. Calling someone "nouveau riche" (newly rich) remains a serious insult in France. An expression has been coined to describe people who show off their wealth: bling-bling. It refers to the noise of the jewels worn by these people.

According to a recent survey, nearly eight out of ten French people feel that being rich is a badly perceived. But on the other hand, nearly three quarters think that it is a praiseworthy thing to want to become rich!

François Hollande said one day: "I don't like rich people," Coming from the mouth of a head of state, the words shocked much of the nation. However, didn't this sentence echo the thoughts of many of his fellow citizens?

Emmanuel Macron has often been pejoratively described as a "president of the rich people," although he has defended himself from being labeled as one.

Nicolas Sarkozy had long time been reproached for the party at the prestigious Fouquet's restaurant on Champs Elysées, just after his election, as well as his vacation on the yacht of a billionaire friend.

Talking about money is still taboo in France, that's a fact. Many sociologists suggest that this is a legacy of French "peasant" culture.

The peasants had cash at home, and one would not talk about it in order to avoid provoking envy, but above all, theft.

It is no doubt that the Catholic religion also has something to do with this. This religion praises poverty and condemns easy money, in contrast to the Protestantism of Anglo-Saxon countries, which are much less guilty for the wealth of its followers.

Others mention the egalitarian and republican dimension of France (another legacy of the Revolution), as being responsible for the money taboo.

In short, one finds in these facts the tortured spirit of the Gauls, always in balance between morality and well-being...

The *"made in France"* concept is also becoming a lure, as more and more companies are outsourcing their production tools to countries where labor costs are much lower than within the borders of ancient Gaul. Many of the former "flagships of French industry" have only their head office in France and all their factories are abroad.

By the way, the majority of French companies are headquartered in Paris or its region, which is also a Gallic characteristic. While our Italian, Spanish, or German neighbors have their economic power centers spread over several cities, in France, everything is largely concentrated, and even congested, in the capital.

General de Gaulle (once again!) rightly referred to "Paris and the French desert." And the trend has not changed since the General's time.

Most French multinationals are managed by a graduate of a *grande école*. And this is once again a local specialty. In 2020, thirty bosses of the CAC 40, the main companies listed on the Paris stock exchange, come from the same nine schools, among which are the indestructible École polytechnique, HEC, or ENA.

I remind you that the École Polytechnique (also called l'X) is an engineering school created during the French Revolution and later "militarized" by Napoleon. This means that, in France, leaders of the largest companies were educated in a military establishment, whose students parade in uniform on the Champs-Élysées on July 14, just like the infantry, cavalry, or parachute regiments! Another curious Gallic specificity...

A similar observation can be made for French politicians, most of whom graduated from the famous École Nationale d'Administration (ENA). What presidents Valéry Giscard d'Estaing, Jacques Chirac, François Hollande, and Emmanuel Macron all have in common is the fact that they graduated from the ENA, albeit at different times.

Is France only led by technocrats?

Is it possible to succeed in France without having a diploma from a prestigious university or school?

Fortunately, yes, and in this respect, and to smile, we can cite the unusual example of Christian Estrosi. This son of Italian immigrants has had a rich political career. President of the region, deputy, secretary of state, minister, and mayor of the city of Nice, this man has held high responsibilities both within his region, the Alpes-Maritimes, and at the national level.

But before entering politics, Christian Estrosi was an excellent motorcycle racer. Carried away by the virus at a very young age, he won the French championship several times and even reached the summits on a world scale.

It is undoubtedly this captivating "first life" that prevented him from continuing his studies, and in particular from passing his baccalaureate.

An interesting anecdote that his political opponents use, not without a certain irony, is that they have often qualified the man, not as an autodidact, but as a motodidact!

Just like Christian Estrosi, despite this "dictatorship of the grandes écoles," there are still some valiant examples of self-taught people in France who have succeeded in both politics and business. However, they are increasingly atypical.

It cannot be denied that French society remains extremely elitist (at least, intellectually speaking). However, access to prestigious schools is a matter of academic success and not of big money, which remains an asset for the nation.

Higher education institutes in France benefit from generous subsidies that make them accessible to almost all scholarships, and without having to go into debt for the rest of one's life. They pride themselves in welcoming more scholarship students year after year. The prize goes to the no less prestigious Institut d'études politiques, where one out of three students does not even have to pay tuition fees!

When you think that in the United States, you have to spend at least thirty thousand dollars a year (if you are not an outstanding sportsman) to pursue any kind of secondary education...

Once again, we can only face the facts: the French are definitely spoiled! In France, all you have to do is work hard at school and be successful at some point...

French education cannot be that bad, since some Gallic graduates are "snatched up." In the all-powerful Silicon Valley, French is the second most spoken language.

For the past few decades, there has even been talk of a worrying brain drain. This is worrying because France is losing its talent and also its public money since the State finances a large part of the education of its graduates, regardless of whether they have followed a public or private curriculum.

The American Grand Canyon, like the country where it took root, continues to fascinate, but the French dream is not so bad either after all.

The École Polytechnique at the head of the military
parade on July 14, as is the tradition.

Image credit: collections École polytechnique / Jérémy Barande

Inventions for the love of sport

We can't really say that the French are a sporting people. Yet, we love sports, but from a rather comfortable position, sitting on a sofa while sipping a beer or a rosé.

France is probably the only country where sports commentators are more famous than the athletes themselves!

I'm exaggerating, of course, but there is some truth in this.

Although they are not perceived as great sportsmen, the French have distinguished themselves by their inventive genius, put at the service of sport.

As mentioned in the chapter on the illustrious Gauls, it is to Baron Pierre de Coubertin that we owe the rebirth of the Olympic Games. For this Parisian aristocrat, the saying *mens sana in corpore sano* (a healthy mind in a healthy body), was transformed into *mens fervida in corpore lacertoso* (a fiery spirit in a muscular body).

It is also thanks to him that we exercise in schools—before restoring the Olympiads of ancient Greece, he fought hard for the introduction of sport in schools in France.

There is a truce of armed conflicts during the Olympic Games. An oath (written by the baron) of fair play, equity and impartiality is pronounced by athletes, referees, and coaches during the opening ceremony. The Olympic flag, made up of five intertwined rings, each representing the five continents united by Olympism, are all Pierre de Coubertin's ideas.

What beautiful symbols! And if French remains one of the two official languages of the International Olympic Committee, it is in tribute to the work of the Parisian baron.

After the Olympic Games, the World Cup is the second most popular sporting event on the planet. And guess who had the idea?

A Gaul!

The Franc-Comtois Jules Rimet, who gave his name to the first trophy, is the main initiator of this competition, which is followed with as much fervor in Tokyo as in Rio de Janeiro.

But waiting four years to follow one's favorite sport can be an excessively long time. So, in 1955, some journalists had the idea to hold a tournament every year between soccer clubs from the same continent. This is how the European Club Cup came into being, and these journalists were... French!

Since it was necessary to reward the best player of the continent, they invented the distinction of the *Ballon d'or* (Golden Ball).

Sixty years after its invention, the trophy still exists and is still extremely coveted. Interest in the European cups has never waned, this is not only true for the public but also for media groups.

And those who hate football are entitled to warmly thank these Frenchmen, all of whom had such wonderful ideas!

One media outlet has played a major role in the popularization of sports in France—the newspaper *L'Équipe*. Many know this four-color daily newspaper, which displays its front pages on newsstands all over the country. What is perhaps less well known is the fact that it belongs to a powerful media group owned by another brotherhood, the Amaury family, a world leader in sporting events organization.

The bike races *Tour de France*, *Paris-Roubaix*, and *Paris-Nice* are theirs. The *Dakar Rally* is still theirs. The *Paris Marathon* and the *French Open Golf Tournament* are also theirs!

The journalists who created the European cups worked at *L'Équipe*, and the *Ballon d'Or* is awarded by *France Football*, a weekly magazine belonging to the same press group.

Another important detail: while our neighbor countries also have several sports newspapers, in France, *L'Équipe* has enjoyed an unquestionable and uncontested monopoly for decades.

A brilliant example of success by crushing all competition!

The *Tour de France* was not created by *L'Équipe*, but by another very popular sports newspaper in its time: *L'Auto*. The jersey color of the leader of this prestigious bicycle race is due to this newspaper since it was printed on yellow paper.

For the anecdote, it is also the case for the Giro of Italy. The beautiful fuchsia pink shirt worn by the first rider of the Giro was strategically chosen to evoke the color of the pages of the transalpine sports daily, *La Gazzetta dello Sport.*

Your humble narrator is an absolute sports fan and an avid reader of *L'Équipe.* My wife often makes fun of me, saying that I can watch a Wimbledon tennis match as passionately as one from the water polo third division.

As for water polo, I tell her that it is due to my interest in horses...

By the way, I am not the only one who loves horses, considering the number of horse sports enthusiasts in France. Once again, we are talking about the French exception.

But in France, if a person watches a horse race, it is, above all, for betting reasons.

Millions of people bet on a horse every year in the hope that it will win a trotting, galloping, or jumping race. Most French cities have racetracks, and some regions of France, such as Normandy, are dedicated to breeding thoroughbreds that will delight their future owners all around the world.

It is a fact that no other country organizes more horse racing criteriums than ancient Gaul, with the most prestigious of them all, the *Prix de l'Arc de Triomphe.*

The origins of horse racing date back to the 6th century. King Bodrick, leader of the Bretons, promised the lucky winner of a galloping contest nothing less than the hand of his daughter, Eleanor! The monarch was firmly convinced that a skilled horseman would make an excellent son-in-law.

It is worth underlining the social mixing that surrounds equestrian sports. Horses are owned by rich personalities, often from the aristocracy. The jockeys are generally middle class (by the way, more and more women are working in this risky profession). And bettors range from the very poor to the very rich. Few sports can boast such a wide range of social status around a similar passion.

A funny story about horse racing: a bettor woke up earlier than expected and noticed that it was exactly 7:07. In the morning, he had an appointment with his banker, who informed him that his account was in credit by 7700 euros. Convinced this was a sign that would bring him luck, he gambled the money he won from the seventh horse in the seventh race of the day.
But the horse came in seventh!

Another Gallic passion is rugby. The oval ball sport is especially very popular in the Anglo-Saxon countries, in particular, the Commonwealth nations. But due to its popularity in France, the local championship enjoys the best reputation.
The English introduced rugby to the city of Le Havre a little more than a hundred years ago, but it is paradoxically in a transversally opposite region, the South-West of France, that it became popular.
Opinions differ as to the reasons for this success, in an area better known for its ocean beaches, forests, and vineyards than its sports fields.

According to some, the massive presence of English merchants and notables in Bordeaux contributed to the propagation of one of their favorite sports, while others believe that the practice of *soule*, an ancient sport very popular in the South-West, made the transition to rugby easier, given the similarities of these two games.

However, these explanations do not seem to convince some historians, who believe that the Great South-West was predisposed to adopt rugby, since strength and physical power are totally part of its local customs, such as the Basque strength tests.

It is often said that soccer is a gentleman's sport supported by hooligans, and that rugby is the opposite. This is not so false, because in France, curiously, rugby is the favorite sport of the aristocracy. For a long time, it was an amateur sport, little tainted by the madness of the fans, festive once the match was over, and it is probably these values that have seduced the followers of "ovalie."

Nevertheless, in the scrum, it is much less friendly. The slap box and the punching factory are fully open...

Although the Frenchies may be not the best athletes, what they are good at is organizing prestigious sporting events in different fields.

I have already underlined the cycling and horse racing competitions, but we can also mention the horsepower races, such as the *Bol d'Or motorcycle race* and the mythical *24 Hours of Le Mans*. This competition is considered one of the three most prestigious races in the world, along with the *Formula 1 Grand Prix in Monaco* and the *Indianapolis 500* in the United States.

Roland-Garros, a century-old tennis tournament, whose final victory, unfortunately, all too often eludes the French, represents another example of the event know-how of ancient Gaul.

And of course, how can we not mention the *World Petanque Championship*?

I am joking, of course. In spite of everything, the passion of the Gauls for what we called colloquially "the bowls" (don't get me wrong, we are still talking about a sport) is very real. It is enough to observe the so many grounds of the country, invested by this so Frenchy game, to understand it.

The history of petanque goes back to the most ancient civilizations, but it is a certain Jules called "Lenoir," native of the city of La Ciotat in the south of France, who defined the rules of the game in 1908, as we know them today.

For the anecdote, the word "pétanque" comes from the patois "pés tanqués," meaning feet together, a position to adopt when you throw the bowl.

In the hearts of the French, perhaps only fishing can compete with petanque.

With its one and a half million members, it is quite simply the second largest sports federation in France in terms of membership, just after soccer.

One might think that fishing is primarily courted by seniors, but think again, a quarter of the members are under 25 years old. A discreet passion which nevertheless brings in more than two billion euros to the Gallic economy...

France is, moreover, the only country in the world to have elected officials running under the political label: *Hunting, fishing, nature, and traditions*—traditions that are fundamentally French!

Between bowls and fishing, how do you expect foreigners not to make fun of the Frenchies, considering their "passion" for sports?

And yet, at each edition of the Olympic Games, so many Gallic athletes do very well. This is certainly true in less mediatized sports, such as archery, rowing, canoeing, BMX, or fencing... But these are legitimate reasons to be proud.

And if France wins, it is also often thanks to its athletes coming from ethnic minorities. For example:

- Tennis player Yannick Noah, whose father was from Cameroon, was the last Frenchman to win the prestigious French Open.
- Zinédine Zidane, whose parents are of Algerian origin, was one of the major architects of the 1998 French national team victory at the soccer world cup.
- Teddy Riner, a native of Guadeloupe, is considered the best *judoka* of all time.
- Tony Parker, French but with an African-American father and a Dutch mother, became the first European to be MVP of a NBA Finals.

And there are so many other examples... So many others that some have found it useful to institute quotas in training centers and soccer schools, with the main objective of limiting the number of French players of African and North African origin, too numerous for their taste.

In other words, and to put it bluntly, they wanted fewer blacks and Arabs on the Gallic fields.

Put simply, this is an ethical and ethnic scandal, totally discriminatory and simply shameful.

In the United States, there are quotas in universities to give more opportunities to minority students. In France, we had the idea to do exactly the opposite!

In fact, we are sometimes so difficult to understand... We are particularly fond of number 2s!

The most representative example is that of the cult devoted to the cyclist Raymond Poulidor, known as "Poupou," who enjoyed exceptional popularity in spite of his status of eternal second on the Tour de France, an event which he never won, but of which he holds the record of podiums.
One goes so far as to speak of a "poupoularity"!
The strangest thing is that, sixty years later, the myth continues as if it were timeless. In a recent survey published by a well-known French daily newspaper, most of the people interviewed considered Raymond Poulidor to be the French cyclist who had the greatest impact on the history of the Tour, ahead of the five-time winners of the event, Jacques Anquetil and Bernard Hinault, which made the latter declare, somewhat bitterly by the

surprising result of the consultation: "In fact, to be popular, it is better to not win the Tour de France!"

In 1984, John McEnroe and Czech-born Ivan Lendl played against each other at the French Open in one of the most epic finals in tennis history. As the American legend was heading towards his first title on the clay court of the French capital, after winning the first two sets, the spectators suddenly started cheering for Lendl, a player who had never really been in the public eye. The support for Lendl was so great that it completely galvanized the Czech (who has since become an American citizen), to the point that he won the match against all odds.

Several years later, the Spanish player, Rafael Nadal, many times winner of the tournament, was victim of the same syndrome. The Parisian public began to support his opponent of the day, Söderling, a Swedish player who was not very well known, to the point that he defeated the Iberian champion in a homeric contest.

There is talk of Stockholm syndrome for hostages who fall in love with their captors. Is there a French syndrome for those who fall in love with losers?

In France, we are capable of anything...

A few decades ago, under the impetus of businessman Bernard Tapie, the football team Olympique de Marseille won everything in its path, including the coveted Champions league (invented by the French) for the first time. Being caught by the anti-corruption patrol regarding a bought match and money hidden in a garden precipitated the fall of the only Frenchy club that was finally winning, and sent its president to jail.

What a mess!

In 2018, the French have once again distinguished themselves, winning the soccer World Cup that took place in Russia. However, the game played by "les Bleus", supposedly unspectacular and very defensive, has never been so criticized... above all by their compatriots!

It would take a long psychoanalysis to explain these astonishing reactions specific to the French.

But how do you put a country on a couch?

In the nineties, when French soccer was at its lowest, it was ironically said that it was so bad that only a foreign club, in this case, Monaco, could win the local French championship.

And still, for Monaco, it is said with slander that unlike other teams, it is the only club where players know the name of their supporters than vice versa!

Laughter is probably the best therapy to combat such a paradox.

Bowls in action in a game of petanque, a game so loved by the French.

The dearest neighbors of the French people

This chapter may be considered polemical (and it may be not the only one), since my words will be based on some generalities.

If I write "the French like the Belgians," there will inevitably be someone who will correct me with the response, "Yes, but not all of them." Not all French people like Belgians...

Therefore, I apologize in advance for these multiple and shameful generalizations, which will nevertheless be the basis of my comments.

After that, if one were content with writing or quoting facts whose accuracy is not in doubt, one would not write or say much more!

In other words, one should not be afraid to throw stones into the pond, but also assume the consequences. On top of that, when one is French, one has a certain DNA of being both a rebel and a provocateur; it's genetic, what can I do?

Preamble completed. Yes, the French like the Belgians!

They like them because they appreciate their kindness, their spontaneity, and perhaps even their innocence and candor. And it is precisely this innocence, candor, and even naivety, which is the basis of the Belgian mocking stories the Frenchies are so fond of.

If there are no more submarines in Belgium, it is because of the open house events.

Forty Belgians were stuck for five hours because an escalator broke down.

These are all good examples of French mockery, sometimes a little cruel, but often benevolent.

The saying "spare the rod and spoil the child" is often used to describe what the Gauls think of "their friends the Belgians." Moreover, this expression, very common in ancient Gaul, is generally badly perceived in Belgium and considered condescending.

The expression *les petits Belges* (the little Belgians) is very popular in France, but much less in the flat country (The French call it this because the highest point is a mountain of 674 meters). And if you add to this that a large part of the world's population thinks that Jacques Brel and Stromae are French, you will understand that on the side of our northern neighbor, one can feel a certain bitterness...

To summarize, the French like the Belgians, but the reciprocal is perhaps not so obvious, and one can easily understand why...

We also have the annoying tendency to systematically associate French fries with the inhabitants of the flat country, whereas it is the Frenchies who invented them!

The fried potato as we know it today, the one that is dipped in fat (preferably twice), is a product born in the streets of Paris, and quoted in the recipe books of two centuries ago.

Moreover, upstream, it is thanks to the tenacity of the pharmacist Antoine Augustin Parmentier that we owe the promotion of the potato since the 18th century. And in English-speaking countries, we speak of French fries, and not Belgian fries!

On this subject, several theories dispute the origin of the term. The first one is precisely, and once again, born from the confusion between Belgians and French. During the Second World War, American soldiers met their Belgian counterparts, who showed them their fries (don't get me wrong, we are still talking about food). Thinking they were French, the GI's returned to Uncle Sam's country with the experience of "French fries" in mind.

According to another hypothesis, in 1802, the President of the United States, Thomas Jefferson, a great lover of Gallic cuisine, asked to be served potatoes in the "French manner." This expression was later adopted by his fellow citizens.

However, you should know that the first exporters of French fries in the world are Belgian. There is no smoke without fire...

When I arrived in Paris, fresh from "my South," the first friend I had was from the Northern city of Lille. Isn't it funny how opposites attract...

Northern France is close to Belgium, and it inevitably rubs off on its citizens. For example, unlike the French, Belgians pronounce the W. Thus, they say Waterloo, not Vaterloo, and Wallon, not Vallon.

One Saturday evening, my new friend and I planned to go to the Champs-Élysées, enjoying the privilege of living in the city where they are located.

The man from Lille gave me an appointment next to the Arc de Triomphe, on the Avenue de Wagram, but pronounced the "Northen way," with a W, not as it should be. After several long minutes spent circling the Place de l'Étoile like a satellite, learning by heart the names of the streets and boulevards that meet there, I realized that the avenue de Wagram was, in fact, the avenue de Vagram, pronounced in the Gallic style... and that my friend was indeed from the north of France!

The relationship between the French and their English neighbors is a little more complicated, and it is a gentle euphemism to say so.

The tone is already set with the "friendly" nicknames we respectively give each other: *Froggies* because, according to the British, the Frenchies love batrachian legs, which they hate, versus *rosbifs*. There are several explanations for the last nickname. The best known meaning of *rosbif* refers to the scarlet skin color of the English, when exposed to a sun they are not used to. Another one is once again culinary. Roast beef is an English invention dating from the 13th century, at a time when meat was still eaten boiled in France. This led the British to assimilate it to their favorite dish. It is worth noting that the word got a bit more French over time to become rosbif.

England is sometimes pejoratively referred to as "perfidious Albion." The expression was first uttered by the 17th century churchman and writer Jacques-Bénigne

Bossuet, who considered that the government of his neighbor across the Channel was regularly in bad faith.

The word albion, which comes from the Latin *albus,* meaning white, has several origins. One of them is geological, since it is a reminder of the white cliffs characteristic of the south coast of England on the approach to Dover from France.

After all, the allusion to the scarlet skin color of the English is not so illegitimate...

Albion is also the Latin name for Great Britain.

We often speak about the "hereditary enemy" on both sides of the Channel. Historically, this is not unjustified in light of the many conflicts between the two countries, one of which lasted almost a hundred years. The so-called "Hundred Years' War" is considered to be the beginning of their military antagonism.

In fact, we have never really managed to understand each other, and this is not only due to a linguistic difference.

We cut off the heads of our kings more than two hundred years ago, while they still worship them.

The French fought alongside the American insurgents against the British colonialists.

We have so often clashed on the different territories where were found each other in Africa, Asia and America.

The Gauls were the originators of Europe, while the British were the first to leave it.

They burned alive our most authentic heroine, Joan of Arc.

We will never understand how you can put jelly in a starter or in a main course.

And I dare not mention sports rivalries.

As a symbol of this recurrent antagonism, the politician Georges Clemenceau, who once declared, not without irony, "What is England? A French colony gone bad."

Conversely, the Francophile, Francophone, and British actor Peter Ustinov uttered this magnificent sentence: "The French and the English were such good enemies that they cannot help but be friends."

And that is certainly what we should remember, because in this historical rivalry, there is, in any case, notable evidence of cooperation and mutual interests.

During the Second World War, England became the antechamber of the French resistance. It was alongside the British that the Americans landed on the beaches of Normandy to liberate France.

Together, we built a magnificent supersonic aircraft, and a gigantic tunnel under the English Channel.

The French have chosen London as their first expatriate destination, which will undoubtedly change with the effects of the Brexit, and British tourists are among the most numerous in France.

In short, it is the expression *"je t'aime, moi non plus"* (I love you, I love you not) that best summarizes the relationship between the British and the French.

Much further south, a mountain range separates us from the Iberians, but it also unites us! The Pyrenees are representative of the relationship between French and Spanish. Often so far away, and yet so close.

As a matter of fact, it was the Treaty of the Pyrenees that put an end to the first conflict between the two countries, which resulted from the Thirty Years' War. In this battle of religious origins that set Europe ablaze in the 17th century, Iberians and Gauls clashed not on their own lands, but in the Netherlands!

One year after the signing of the treaty, Louis XIV married with great fanfare, and ironically, at the foot of the Pyrenees mountain range in Saint-Jean-de-Luz, the infanta of Spain, and incidentally, his first cousin. As a dowry, France got back the Roussillon, the Artois (today the department of Pas-de-Calais), and part of Lorraine returned by the kingdom of Spain. The cardinal Mazarin, in charge at that time, conducted skillful negotiations.

A few years later, Louis XIV (again) took advantage of a new war of succession across the Pyrenees to install his grandson, the Duke of Anjou, on the Spanish throne.

To conclude this historical aside, the latest antagonism between the two countries is wonderfully illustrated in Francisco de Goya's painting, *Tres de mayo*, which can be admired at the Prado Museum in Madrid. It depicts a shooting of rebels by Napoleonic troops, following the anti-Goya uprising of May 2, 1808. This was a time when the French emperor took advantage of the political instability in the peninsula to send his older brother Joseph (renamed "Pepe botella" by the Iberians because of his alleged love of alcoholic beverages) to rule the kingdom.

So in fact we only had three conflicts with our Spanish neighbors—very few in a Europe where nations have never stopped fighting each other.

Examples of cooperation are much more representative about the joint history of our two nations. During the civil war, many Iberian republicans found refuge in the border country. In the midst of Franco's dictatorship, the Spaniards saw their northern neighbor as a more suitable place to find work. As a result, in France many people have Garcia, Fernandez, Lopez, or Sanchez as a surname.

The French admire their Spanish neighbors for their epicurean lifestyle, which is similar to their own. *Fiesta, comida, bebida*: the two peoples have common values, and this is probably why Spain is the favorite destination for French vacationers. The reciprocal is true since the majority of Iberians also go on vacation in France. By the way, both countries are the most visited on our planet.

However, there are still some areas of friction. The Iberians are formidable competitors in agriculture. Some of Spain's top restaurants have nothing to envy when it comes to their Gallic counterparts. The fishermen of the peninsula and those of France are constantly engaged in small wars. And the cava from Catalonia is stepping on the toes of the cheap champagnes...

With Catalan and Basque claims to independence ever increasing, Spain faces a crucial geopolitical challenge in the coming years. But Catalonia and the Basque Country are not only in Spain... No doubt France will also be concerned by what happens on the other side of the Pyrenees, the unity of these two nations is at stake!

Since I have been living in Spain for twenty years, I had so many stories and anecdotes to tell that I wrote a book. However, I failed to tell this other anecdote about the confusions generated by pronunciation errors, this time in the French-Spanish direction.

Janitors are still present in the old buildings of the Iberian capital. The janitor of the first apartment where I lived in Madrid was called Ramon, an excellent person, always ready to help.

It turns out that for many weeks I renamed Ramon to Jamon, which is pronounced almost identically, but does not mean quite the same thing. In other words, I called someone named Raymond, Ham!

When a French-Spanish friend walked me back to my apartment once greeted the janitor, he called me out with these words:

"Do you realize that you just called him: ham?"

The providential friend reminded me of the necessity to roll the "r" properly in order to pronounce this name correctly, and thus avoid a perilous misunderstanding. And since Ramon was such a lovely person, he had never dared to make the remark before...

Jean Cocteau once said: "The Italians are good-tempered French." One can contest this negative perception of the French on their "good or bad" mood, but Cocteau's vision on the similarity of the two peoples deserves reflection.

First, we have so much in common with them.

The roots of our language, the love of art, and singularly, a common history.

In France, Julius Caesar is well known as Vercingetorix. Napoleon III has more street names in "the boot" than in the ancient Gaul.

The Italian Garibaldi is also considered a hero in France. The city of Nice and the region of Savoy have only been French since 1860.

Provence owes its name to the Transalps for having been one of their provinces for so long.

The *Pont du Gard*, the city of Vaison-la-Romaine, the buildings: *Maison Carrée* in Nîmes *and Porte de Mars* of Reims, the Lutetia Arena in Paris, the ancient theater of Orange: the Romans have left so many traces of their passage in Gaul that one could almost speak of another Italy.

And then, the Italians make the Gauls laugh so much, thanks to their way of being, because of their glibness, and thanks to their efforts of always looking good.

During a trip to Lombardy, after landing at Malpensa airport near Milan, the vision of the marshaler in charge of guiding the aircraft to the terminal made me laugh out loud. Ray-Ban sunglasses, an Armani neckerchief, and a beautifully trimmed three-day beard. No doubt about it, I had indeed arrived in Italy!

There is undeniably a French fascination for the country of commedia dell'arte, of the dolce vita, of La Scala, of Venice, of Rome, but also of the mafia and schemes of all kind. As mentioned in the chapter on love, Silvio Berlusconi could have been a president that the French would have loved to have!

We affectionately call the Italians *ritals,* and a little less delicately *macaroni* or *spaghetti.*

For the record, the word rital would come from Italian resident/refugee, written *R-Ital* on the documents of transalpine emigrants who arrived in France at the beginning of the 20th century. But according to another source, the word rital comes from the inscriptions on the trains that repatriated Italians in the 1920s—the *rapatriés italiens*.

Ungrudgingly and much more elegantly, the Transalps use the expression "our French cousins" to define their northern neighbors.

If France was invaded by ancient Rome two thousand years ago, many other waves of Italian immigration have followed since. First in the Middle Ages, then during the Renaissance, but particularly from the second half of the 19th century. As France lacked the manpower to support its growth and could not count on neighboring countries such as Belgium, Switzerland, or Germany, which were also in need of expatriates, the Italians were welcome. Waves of transalpine emigration to France followed one after the other during the 20th century, depending on economic and political events, with Fascism causing a considerable number of Italians to flee.

Nowadays, the French population of Italian descent is estimated at some four million people! As matter of fact, in France, everyone has friends with transalpine ancestors.

The Belgian novelist Paul Carvel wrote, "Sign language is useful for the deaf but vital for Italians." So, to finish on this subject, let's quote this slightly mocking anecdote about an Italian prisoner. Handcuffed and ordered to speak, he replied, "I am sorry, I can't speak without my hands free. I am Italian."

Let's go a little further north to talk about Switzerland, or rather the Swisserlands, since there are several of them. Obviously it is the French-speaking part that the French know best.

A German journalist once wrote, "What separates the Germans from the Austrians is that they speak the same language." A similar quote would almost apply to the French and Swiss, since they have so little in common.

While the Gaul is a born rebel against his government or his administration, the Swiss are disciplined and have full confidence in their elected representatives.

In the Swiss Confederation, employees can be fired without cause. The Swiss work 42 hours a week and enjoy five weeks of vacation. They start their day at 7:00 am and finish at 5:00 p.m. sharp, and it is frowned upon to stay afterwards as it means that the person is inefficient in his or her work.

By all means, in France, we have a very different view and organization style.

In the Confederation, there is no occupational medicine, no trade union delegates, no works council, no reimbursement of transport costs, no luncheon vouchers. Social security companies are private, there is no gender parity in political life, and military service is compulsory for men.

Believe me when I write that the French are lucky people!

The Helvetians are considerably patriotic. In a typical house in Switzerland, one frequently finds a Swiss flag, and sometimes garden gnomes (the two objects having nothing to do with each other).

If in France, the garden gnome is tolerated, the tricolor flag in his garden is perceived as a fascist symbol!

In the Confederation, there is no need to punch a public transport ticket, and referendums are held on surprising subjects such as the presence of minarets, the free trade agreement with Bulgaria and Romania, or the financing of invalidity insurance.

So, are you convinced that we don't have much in common with our Swiss friends?

Moreover, we have been annoying them in recent years, due to a massive arrival of Gallic expatriates, who come to find work in their neighboring countries that their country of birth is no longer able to offer them.

To counter this competition, there has been an upsurge in the number of mentions of "Swiss and Swiss residence" in the selection criteria of job ads on the Lake Geneva side.

According to some sources, an anti-French sentiment is singularly felt around. The Swiss even use the pejoratives words Frouzes or Shadoks to refer to their neighbors.

I recall that the Shadoks are these somewhat intellectually limited creatures, from a mythical French television program...

And the French do the same, castigating the supposed slowness of the Swiss and systematically associating them with the stereotypes of banker, watchmaker, fondue, knife or chocolate!

For chocolate, the giant Nestlé, whose headquarters are in Switzerland, is certainly a factor.

French companies have also used the "Swiss" brand extensively, sometimes without any connection with the country.

Les 3 Suisses is known for being a mail order catalog, spanning generations and published in the north of France. *Petit-suisse* is a delicious fresh cheese made in... Normandy!

It is interesting to note that "Swiss knife" has become a synonym in France for a multidisciplinary person who can do everything!

To close this chapter on what the French think of other nations, limited to the big border countries, otherwise a new book would be needed, and also because if I continue, I will not make only friends. Let's refer to Germany.

At the dawn of the third millennium, the powerful eastern neighbor is probably the closest ally to France. One even goes so far as to speak of a "Franco-German couple."

There are countless examples of cooperation between the two countries, from the setting up of European Union to the assembly of Airbus planes and soon high-speed trains. We even jointly created a cultural television channel (Arte) and an Office for Youth Cooperation (OFAJ). January 22, the anniversary of the 1963 Elysée Treaty, which sealed the reconciliation, is now a Franco-German day.

Such a long way has come for these former enemies, and this is great to see. French people passionately followed the events that led to the fall of the Berlin Wall and the reunification of the country. This undeniably increased the sympathy capital of the Germans for the Gauls. Another paradox of history!

Germany is France's economic model. It is France's number one trading partner, its number one supplier, and also its number one customer. When Germany coughs, France gets the flu, and if the Germans are doing well, the French are doing just fine.

Made in Germany is a popular choice among French people. Whether they dress in Adidas, Puma, or Hugo Boss, take care of their bodies with Nivea creams, or dream of Mercedes, BMW or Porsche sedans.

Berlin is seen by many French as a "trendy" city, a cultural crossroads of Europe, but also the perfect place to start a business. More and more Frenchy entrepreneurs are moving to the German capital to set up their start-ups.

The Gauls admire the organization, order, discipline, civic-mindedness, and punctuality of their eastern neighbors. Exactly what they lack, but also what they most often hate...

However, can we talk about the ideal, dreamed, perfect country on the French side?

Maybe not...

In ancient Gaul, there is certainly an admiration and a deep respect for the Germanic nation, but the country of

Goethe is not the one that we will take familiarly under our arm...

While there is a real closeness of lifestyle with the Italians and Spaniards, with the Germans, it is a little different. The French are a Latin people with a frivolous, libertine, sometimes undisciplined, disorderly culture, far from Germanic standards.

Moreover, we often have so much trouble understanding each other.

Consider the accounts of some German personalities splashed by tax evasion cases denouncing themselves. Such was the case of the former president of Bayern Munich, Uli Hoeness, who, after having reimbursed part of the embezzled sum, went to prison himself!

In France, a similar fact would never happen.

Volkswagen's "dieselgate" certainly demonstrated that German ethics are not above reproach. Nevertheless, the reaction of the industrial group was admirable, with the immediate resignation of the main executives and the payment of the fine in full.

The circumstances are certainly different, but at the same time, the former CEO of Renault-Nissan was accused in Japan of failure to declare income and breach of trust. Deceiving the vigilance of his guards, he fled under a fictitious identity and by private plane, after a fantastic escape worthy of a James Bond movie, to land in Lebanon.

The sense of humor between Gauls and Germans is also not quite similar. While French jokes are mostly based on making fun of others, Germans tend to laugh at themselves or at a situation.

In 2006, an advertising campaign of the airline Air Berlin caused a sensation, offering unbeatable tickets with the slogan: "We are not joking, we are German."

What a sense of self-mockery!

And since we are in the business of self-mockery, let's stay with it, to mention this anecdote that turns out to be true.

A young child discovered his Christmas present and was inconsolable. His grandfather, who was in charge of playing Santa Claus for the occasion, was moved by his grandson's reaction and did not understand the reasons for his sadness. His son took him aside to explain that he had bought the book *Mein Kampf*, while his child was dreaming of the game *Minecraft*.

The words sounded almost the same, but the result was very different...

Major subject of a clash between the French and the Belgians.
If it stays like this, nobody will complain!

Gratitude

Thank you, dear readers, for reading my book! If I could make you laugh, teach you a few things, but above all make you have a good time, then know that I will be very happy. It will be for me the most beautiful reward.

Thank you to France, a country I love so much, even though I have been unfaithful to it for more than a quarter of a century. I will repeat it once again: if I had not been French, so much would I have liked to be...

Thank you to my parents for everything. I was so lucky to have you.

Thank you to my brother for all his precious advice.

Thank you to my wife for her unconditional love (I'm exaggerating a bit here...) and for tolerating the water polo matches!

Thanks to my children Jon and Clara, for sometimes putting up with my absences.

And...

Thanks to God, Allah, Javeh, Dios, the source...

Be happy, and put love in the center of your life...

This is the only true thing.

We are only made to love!

From the same author

If you have enjoyed *Everything you always wanted to know about the French*, then maybe you will also like: *Everything you always wanted to know about the Spanish*.

Why are Spaniards so close (in every sense of the word) to their families?

How do they handle work, parties, and naps so well?

What is the source of their surprising love of sport?

Is religion still so influential in Spain?

Why do the Spanish love to gossip so much?

What are the secrets of Cervantes' language?

What is happening to the Catalans?

Why is there such a passion for Spanish gastronomy nowadays?

These and other questions are answered in this book through amusing anecdotes and real-life experiences.

Everything you always wanted to know about the Spanish* (*but were afraid to ask)

A social-historical-humorous essay on the Spanish people

Gaspard Chevallier

I created my own company

Case study of entrepreneurship

Gaspard Chevallier

And in French...

Bienvenue chez les Gaulois

Essai socio-historico-humoristique pour mieux comprendre les Français

Gaspard Chevallier

Bienvenue chez les Ibériques

*L'Espagne dans tous ses états,
sous la plume amusée d'un Français expatrié*

Gaspard Chevallier

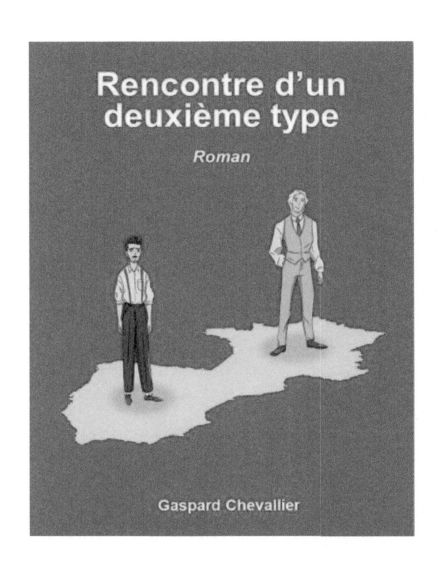

Data sources

All the French people (of which I am also a part) who I have met or observed. They are the main inspiration for this book.

The French media, I have read them with a different eye, listened to them from another perspective, and watched them in depth in order to better understand the secrets of my country.

The great, magnificent, and so useful internet web, and more precisely, the following articles and references:

Article by Pascal Riché published on May 25, 2013 in *L'obs- avec rue99*
https://www.nouvelobs.com/rue89/rue89-rue89-culture/20130525.RUE6483/neuf-choses-que-vous-ne-savez-sans-doute-pas-sur-jeanne-d-arc.html
http://thaloe.free.fr/francais/historic1.html

"The French are the most arrogant in Europe according to...the French" published in Le HuffPost on May 15, 2013 for huffingtonpost.fr
https://www.huffingtonpost.fr/2013/05/15/francais-plus-arrogants-europe-selon-francais_n_3277489.html

Article by Julie Piérart published in Babbel magazine " the origins of the French language ", March 8, 2017.
https://fr.babbel.com/fr/magazine/histoire-du-francais

Article published in *L'express* by Michel Feltin-Palas, September 3, 2019 "Paris is no longer the leading French-speaking city in the world"
https://www.lexpress.fr/culture/paris-n-est-plus-la-premiere-ville-francophone-du-monde_2096093.html

Article by Ilyes Zouar published May 15, 2017 in *Les Échos* "Paris is no longer the leading French-speaking city in the world"
https://francophonie-avenir.com/fr/Info-breves/231-Paris-n-est-plus-la-premiere-ville-francophone-du-monde

Article by Anne-Cécile S. published on May 23, 2016 in *Franchement bien* "the bikini is a French invention"
https://franchementbien.fr/le-bikini-une-invention-francaise/

Article published in *Futura Sciences*, undated and unsigned: "Who are the main philosophers of the Enlightenment?
https://www.futura-sciences.com/sciences/questions-reponses/histoire-sont-principaux-philosophes-lumieres-5625/

Article published in *pourquoi.com* undated and unsigned: "Why do we play more rugby in the South West?"
https://www.pourquois.com/inclassables/pourquoi-joue-plus-rugby-dans-sud-ouest.html

Article by Claire Jenik's on August 08, 2019, "The French, champions of time spent eating"
https://fr.statista.com/infographie/13223/heures-minutes-passees-manger-et-boire-ocde/

Article published in *Le point* on July 7, 2017 "Food critic Christian Millau, co-founder of "Gault et Millau," has died
https://www.lepoint.fr/societe/le-critique-gastronomique-christian-millau-cofondateur-du-gault-et-millau-est-decede-07-08-2017-2148516_23.php

Article published by Marcel Gay on January 5, 2020 "Will we still be speaking French in 50 years?
https://infodujour.fr/culture/8988-parlera-t-on-encore-francais-dans-50-ans

Article published by Blandine Lamorisse in *La République du centre* on February 5, 2018 "Stars, plates, cutlery... The vocabulary of the Michelin Guide deciphered"
https://www.lejdc.fr/nevers-58000/actualites/etoiles-assiettes-couverts-le-vocabulaire-du-guide-michelin-decrypte_12728362/
http://www.fromage-france.fr/

Article published in *Science&vie* by Adeline Colonat on September 30, 2017 "Is red wine really good for the heart?"
https://www.science-et-vie.com/questions-reponses/le-vin-rouge-est-il-vraiment-bon-pour-le-coeur-9620

Article published in *La-Philo*, undated and unsigned
https://la-philosophie.com/philosophie-lumieres

Article by La Brinvilliers on May 17, 2019, in History for all of France and the world "The discovery of the Venus de Milo"
https://www.histoire-pour-tous.fr/arts/2985-la-venus-de-milo.html

Article published by Laurent Guez on June 24, 2014 in *Les Echos* "the French and money, complicated relations"
https://www.lesechos.fr/2015/06/les-francais-et-largent-des-relations-compliquees-266832

Article published by Nadasto on 18 February 2014 "The differences between Cognac and Armagnac"
http://gourmandisesansfrontieres.fr/2014/02/les-differences-entre-le-cognac-et-larmagnac/

Article written by Stéphane.B on 25 September 2015 "Five differences between cognac and armagnac"
http://www.cognacprunier.fr/blog/article26/5-differences-entre-le-cognac-et-l-armagnac

Article published in *La Croix* by Mireille Hadas-Lebe on May 28, 2015 " The Jews of France: some lessons from history"
https://www.la-croix.com/Urbi-et-Orbi/Archives/Documentation-catholique-n-2520-E/Les-juifs-de-France-quelques-lecons-de-l-histoire-2015-05-28-1317025

Article published by Blandine Le Cain on April 10, 2013 in *Le Figaro* "Why do the French have trouble talking about money?"
https://www.lefigaro.fr/actualite-france/2013/04/10/01016-20130410ARTFIG00896-pourquoi-les-francais-ont-ils-du-mal-a-parler-d-argent.php

Article published in *Ensemble-en-france.org* undated and unsigned "Why is talking about money taboo in France?"
https://www.ensemble-en-france.org/pourquoi-parler-dargent-est-tabou-en-france/

Article published by VL in *France Soir* on December 11, 2014 "why the Marseillaise is called that"
http://www.francesoir.fr/culture-musique/pourquoi-la-marseillaise-sappelle-t-elle-ainsi

Article published in *Paris zig zag*: "What is the oldest monument in Paris?
https://www.pariszigzag.fr/secret/histoire-insolite-paris/plus-vieux-monument-parisien

Article by Jean-Baptiste Pasquier: "The true history of pastis!" published in *Le petit ballon* on 18 July 2019
https://www.lepetitballon.com/blog/histoire-pastis.html

Article from Pierre Ménager undated
https://www.uneautremarseillaisepourlafrance.fr/blog/2015/12/le-sang-impur-de-la-marseillaise-na-jamais-ete-celui-des-francais/

Article published on June 16, 2017 "Why are French fries "French fries" in our English-speaking neighbors?" http://mccain.begooddogood.fr/pourquoi-les-frites-sont-elles-des-french-fries-chez-nos-voisins-anglo-saxons/

Article published on March 12, 2017 by Christine Mateus in *Le Parisien* "fishing sport superstar" http://www.leparisien.fr/societe/loisirs-la-peche-sport-superstar-12-03-2017-6754746.php

Article published on June 28, 2013 by Polyglotcoach in *Polyglottes*: "Oh là là! Let's lift the mystery on this mythical French expression" https://polyglottes.org/2013/06/28/oh-la-la/

The cover of this book was created with the drawings of Akia Louh, a very talented artist.

Printed in Great Britain
by Amazon

21500698R00103